IF I KNEW THEN

Finding wisdom in failure
and power in aging

JANN ARDEN

RANDOM HOUSE CANADA

PUBLISHED BY RANDOM HOUSE CANADA

www.penguinrandomhouse.ca

LIBRARY AND ARCHIVES CANADA CATALOGUING IN PUBLICATION

Title: If I knew then : finding wisdom in failure and power in aging / Jann Arden.
Names: Arden, Jann, author.
Identifiers: Canadiana (print) 20200192361 | Canadiana (ebook) 202001924oX
| ISBN 9780735279971 (hardcover) | ISBN 9780735279988 (EPUB)
Subjects: LCSH: Arden, Jann. | LCSH: Singers—Canada—Biography. |
LCSH: Actresses—Canada—Biography. | LCSH: Aging. | LCGFT: Autobiographies.
Classification: LCC ML420.A676 A3 2020 | DDC 782.42164092—dc23

Cover and text design: Terri Nimmo
Image credits: (cover photo) © Alkan Emin; (spine) Yulia Reznikov/Getty Images

Printed and bound in Canada

10 9 8 7 6 5 4 3 2 1

Penguin
Random House
RANDOM HOUSE CANADA

To my parents,

Joan and Derrel Richards.

Contents

I AM
A
CRONE ♡

Waiting for the Crone

THE MEANING OF the word *crone* varies depending on the person using it. Wikipedia says she is almost always a character in folklore and fairy tales. She is usually very disagreeable, somewhat sinister and malicious, with a sprinkling of magical or supernatural powers. That all sounds completely delicious to me. She sounds like somebody I'd like to invite over for a few pots of Earl Grey tea and a platter of carbohydrates.

I didn't know who I was going to become in my forties or my fifties, I really didn't. My twenty-year-old self just threw her head back and laughed at the thought of being that old. But I'm starting to get a clear picture of who I am going to be as I march into my sixties and seventies, Goddess willing!

JANN ARDEN

Although the word itself is often associated
with being aged and ugly and mean-spirited, to me
a Crone is a kick-ass, take-no-prisoners, damn-the-
torpedoes, own-your-own-crap, great kind of person
to be. Entering into the time of the Crone, for me and
thousands of other women (and perhaps a few fortunate
men), has been nothing short of extraordinary.

The Crone is remarkably wise and unapologetic.
She is fierce and forward-thinking—someone who
is at the pinnacle of her own belonging. Okay, I'm not
entering the time of the Crone, I *am* a Crone. I am at the
beginning of a new chapter in my life—a whole new
book, really. And it's one that's going to read and
unfold exactly the way I want it to.

The first Crones I ever met were my grandmothers.
As I was growing up, I watched both of them evolve into
such fierce women, reaching for their "Crone-ness"
in their own unique ways. I was both enamoured of
them and a tiny bit afraid at the same time. I didn't
know it then, but Crones don't take crap from anyone,
even their own grandchildren.

My great-aunts were Crones too. My great-aunt
Earn, who was her mother's namesake, was a force to
be reckoned with. She was a journalist before women

were even trying to be journalists. She drove around in a little sports car like she was in the Indy 500, and I'm pretty sure she didn't even have a driver's licence, nor did she care. She smoked roll-your-own cigarettes, drank whiskey and swore with a great deal of purpose. She was one of the most unforgettable women I have ever met. She married, but very much on her own terms, and she never stopped working. When she got cancer in her early eighties, she remained unflinchingly calm, cool and collected. She wore a wig when her hair fell out after what was the first and last round of cancer treatment (sadly, it did not work), and I watched her chuck it into a roaring fire at a family reunion as she exclaimed, "I'm ready to die, but it sure as hell isn't an easy thing to do!"

I recall it bursting into a ball of colourful flames and making a searing noise, and everybody laughing and slapping their knees. It was a good day for all of us, but not so good for the wig.

I remember listening to my mom's mom and her sisters telling stories about their lives when they all got together. Rings of smoke circled their heads and stubby beer bottles were plunked on the table between decks of cards and tins of tobacco. Those old stories seemed to fill them with power and confidence. I miss all of them more than you could ever know. I miss their cackles and their beautiful wrinkled faces and their gnarled hands waving in the air as they laughed and laughed and laughed.

How I looked forward to having stories of my own to tell!

My maternal grandmother, Clara, talked about time a lot, how time made sense of things and how time handed out wisdom. She told me I would have to wait to be wise, that nothing made you wise but time. I understand that now.

In my eight-year-old brain, I did sometimes wonder if they had ever been young. It felt to me as if they had always been these aged marvels—smart and sure and steady—and *old*. I realize now that they were probably much like me when they were young—unsure, tentative, hesitant. It takes a long time to become a person. I wish they were here right now to inform me and help me and guide me . . . But I'm pretty sure they are, right here in my head and heart, doing just that. I have to stop and be still long enough to hear them.

—

Lots of us don't know quite what to expect as we grow older. It's shrouded in our fear and worry about what we see as the inevitable decline. When we do think about it, we imagine it's all about closing up shop or slowing things down or wrapping up loose ends. We think about the wrinkles that slither onto our brows and hands and necks, and we want all that to stop. We want to have our necks back, and our firm, strong legs and arms, and we want to have endless energy, and we want all of our marbles to stay right where they are!

But honestly, I have found such kindness in my bones as I have aged, an acceptance of self that I didn't even know existed. I'm simply not hard on myself anymore. I appreciate the fact that my body is carting my soul around and it's doing a spectacular job of it. I see such strength and ability in myself, which I didn't even notice, let alone appreciate, when I was a young woman. I didn't know how.

What I think about now couldn't be further from brooding on time running out. Instead, I'm focused on reimagining and reinvention, the act of becoming someone I always hoped I would be. I feel that I am a wise woman emerging through the trees with a renewed sense of the purpose of my own glorious life.

Now that I'm a Crone, I speak my mind and chase my passions relentlessly. I do not need to wait for permission from anyone to do as I please, and I throw my opinions around, not like confetti, but like lightning bolts. Opinions and thoughts and ideas that are bigger than the whole of the sun—and why not?

To finally be at a place in my life where I value my body (most of the time—I slip up some days) and my heart and my mind in equal measure is still remarkable to me, unbelievable to me, but this is what is happening. The passage of time brings with it an unmistakable wonder. It brings a culmination of all the experiences that led me here, to this rock on which I stand—a rock of my own making.

Youth has its delicate wonder, its mischief and tender innocence, but there is little power in the handful of experiences of youth. We Crones have piled up thousands of undertakings over the years, and they provide us with a majestic view: a view of our own life, a view that enables us to be fair and kind and supportive of ourselves and each other.

I would be remiss if I did not add that, occasionally, very young Crones walk the planet. I have met some incredibly brave ten-year-old girls who have taught me a thing or two. There are some very old souls among us who defy all the rules and everyone's expectation of what a ten- or twelve- or fifteen-year-old girl should know and can be.

So here I am, a full-on Crone, or at least well on my way to being one. I'm letting her take over my body with every decision I make, every choice, every conversation, every job I undertake. It feels right. It feels decadent and incredibly good. I am learning to listen, really listen to the voice inside my heart and head. I don't ignore that voice the way I used to when I was young. I used to override every sage bit of advice I gave myself, mainly because I didn't feel worthy. At last I can tell you without hesitation that I feel worthy of good things happening to me.

If I am lucky— Ugh, forget lucky, luck has nothing to do with anything; it's all hard work and dedication and steadfastness, period. As I keep working towards myself, I look forward to the old face that (I hope) will look back at me from a mirror someday. I see new wrinkles pretty much on a weekly basis—new marks, new spots. I see them and feel grateful just to be here. Many of my friends and family members are not. They left far too early, and I miss them all terribly. You feel that your pack gets smaller as you get older, as all the souls you've been travelling with break away and head back into the abyss. It's weird and kind of wonderful to think I might join up with them again someday. Even as molecules spinning in the ether.

Getting older in this life is a privilege.

It's not the enemy at all—it's a damn adventure. You've got a ticket to that adventure, so be daring and spontaneous and brave.

Mom used to say, "If you can't be brave, be reckless." I miss her the very most.

1. Dying is a five-letter word. (This was one of my mother's favourite sayings, and I'm not sure to this day what the joke was. I think it was a riff on bad words usually being four letters long, combined with people's reluctance to talk about dying. This is a very long chapter title.)

You're going to die someday. My mother told me that when I was eight or nine years old. *You're going to die, so you had better get on with your life and make it a good one.*

In the last few years, as I watched both my parents leave this life, I've thought a lot about how blunt she was with me at such a young age, and why. I have no idea really, except that she didn't seem to fear death the way most of us do. She never said a single thing about being afraid of dying. "For one thing, Jann, I'm not ever going to know I'm dying, so why would I be afraid of that?"

The reason I tell you this is that my mother was the epitome of a Crone. Don't get me wrong, she certainly had fears, but they were reasonable ones. My mom wanted me to get on with living and taking chances and being bold and brave and trying things out even if I failed at them. That was the message that came through for me as I got older. My mom wanted me to know that there was a time limit to life and that that was okay. It wasn't something I should waste my time lamenting over—death, that is. I should spend my time and energy on living life, not thinking about its end. When you're young, you waste time because you think it's limitless, and my mother wanted me to understand from day one that time would eventually run out.

My dad, on the contrary, lived his entire life worrying about dying. He was always so afraid of it. To be honest, it was rather heartbreaking. He was the first of my parents to go and he was very reluctant to leave this earth. It took him many days of laboured breathing—heaving, actually, deep, guttural heaving— that left me and my brother completely horrified. My mother was already living within the blur of her Alzheimer's disease (even though she hadn't been diagnosed) and wasn't completely "there" in the room while Dad was dying. She sat in a corner clutching her purse and repeatedly asking my brother Patrick if it would "kill someone to get your father a lozenge."

She figured a lozenge would solve all his problems. It was one of the few moments we actually laughed out loud. Her Alzheimer's was a gift that day, because she didn't know what was actually happening.

As I listened to him struggle, I didn't know whether to run down the hallway and scream for help (which seems like the thing you *should* do when someone is dying, GET HELP) or start CPR myself, based on what I'd learned watching Chad Everett on *Medical Center* in the 1970s.

But that's not what happens when someone is dying. You sit at the side of an adjustable bed that nobody who isn't a trained professional knows how to adjust and watch someone you love (well, in my dad's case, someone you sort of love, but don't really like much at all) breathe in and out as if their lungs are filled with gravel and Vaseline. There was a brief moment when I thought we had actually murdered my father by "folding" him into the bed we clearly had no idea how to operate. I had just wanted to prop his head up a little to ease his breathing, but instead we managed to turn him into a human taco. The nurse glared at me when she came into the room, saying, "We would prefer it if you'd come to us directly for any adjustments."

I loved

my dad

but I didn't always
like him —

For the last few hours of his life my dad's eyes were focused on some invisible hole in the ceiling. I kept asking him what he was looking at, but he did not respond to my queries. His pupils were the smallest of specks, as though they were filled with a light bigger and brighter than the sun. Every so often his gasping would stop. I can't ever remember being more frightened.

ARE YOU DEAD, DAD? The voice in my head echoed as if I was shouting into the Grand Canyon.

Dead silence.

Stillness.

My brother, my mother and I all stood up from our crappy plastic chairs and leaned over him, peering down into his face, trying to assess what was going on. We didn't know what we were doing. There was no one helping us, or guiding us, or telling us what to expect. It was awful.

"I think he's gone," my brother finally said, and tears started to stream down his pale face. "Yeah, he's gone this time—I think . . ."

"I don't know, Pat, that's what you said last time."

And then Dad would jerk and gulp in a gigantic mouthful of air and we'd jump out of our exhausted, horrified skins. It went on like that for hours.

And then, when it was over, truly over, there was no mistaking what had happened. We felt him go. It was something very tactile. The sudden emptiness made you wonder if maybe you were dead too. We all stood there looking down at him, looking at his shell. Mom used to say that your soul was your pilot and your body was your spaceship, and now Dad's spaceship had nobody inside it. He was so gone I wondered how he had ever been in there at all.

"We should tell somebody," I said.

"Yeah, okay," Pat answered quietly. "I'll go."

I hoped he wouldn't find the dour nurse who got mad because I adjusted the bed.

While Pat was gone, I tried to get my dad's eyelids to shut. That's what you're supposed to do, right? Gently close the dead person's eyes. But he hadn't blinked in the five or six hours before he passed. I am not exaggerating: he did not blink. So his eyes were beyond dry, the lids folded back like tiny accordions. I pulled them down ever so gently and they simply popped back open.

HE'S ALIVE AGAIN!

The thought shot through my head like a paper cut. Those quick, vicious paper cuts that always catch you so off guard.

I tried again, and one more time, but I could not get them to close.

When Pat came back into the room, he had a nurse in tow who was happily not the grumpy, officious one. She took out her stethoscope and listened to a few spots on Dad's chest. She checked his pulse. She shone a little light back and forth across his eyes.

"He has passed away," she said, and turned around and left.

We weren't sure what we were supposed to do next, and the nurse hadn't offered any suggestions, which I thought was odd. I suppose it was all routine for her, but we were first-timers in the dying parent department and could have used a little guidance.

My brother cried a lot, but I just stood there at the end of the bed like an old tree. My mom didn't cry or call out or throw herself over the body of her husband of fifty-seven years. She just sat there with her purse clutched to her chest.

She asked Patrick what was wrong with him, because he was crying so hard, and he told her point-blank, "Dad died."

She said, "Well, he completely ruined my birthday."

I'm not kidding. My mom didn't remember how to work a toaster anymore, but she knew it was her seventy-ninth birthday. We couldn't believe it.

My dad died on my mother's birthday. Mainly because he didn't want us to forget him, I'm sure. He wasn't someone you would ever easily forget. Eventually I realized I was looking down at Dad with relief because my headache was gone. I had never in my life had a headache until my head decided it was going to try to explode as I was watching my dad die. Stress, fear, anxiety. All of the above. When I think about it now, I'm pretty sure my headache was a reaction to his soul coming in and out of my body, struggling to be in one plane of existence or the other. I don't care how nutty that sounds, because that is exactly what it felt like. His soul was a wave of energy and I felt it/him—and not in a good way. It hurt.

At the very second he bolted out of his extremely tired body, my headache began to lift. Within two or three minutes it was gone. I felt no pain, just a dull fatigue and an emptiness that had no motion or sound or light.

You're going to die someday, so make your life a good one.

I think my dad spent so much of his life worrying about dying that he missed out on living it. I really do. I am pretty sure that's why my mom made the effort to direct all us kids into a different way of thinking. I wish my dad had had an easier time of it, but wishing is an empty thing. You have to act upon a wish to make it come true, and he never did.

My mother's death three years later, in early 2019, was completely different except for one thing: the headache that pushed itself out through my eye sockets. It was so bad I thought I was having an aneurism, a fear that made my heart smash around in my rib cage like a frantic sparrow. My second headache in fifty-six years.

Unlike my dad, Mom was relaxed and peaceful and determined to get going. I took some solace in the fact that she was clearly done with Planet Earth. She knew what she was doing, and she was determined and forthright and steadfast. The curse of Alzheimer's is also the blessing of Alzheimer's: there's a mental vacuum that allows you to be unaware of everything that's happening to you. Yet, as I write these words, I realize she was very aware of leaving. She was so purposeful I was filled with wonder. I was so proud of her. It was her last earthly task, and she was fully in control. It was the rest of us who were all over the place and wondering what the hell to do. Nobody teaches you how to act when someone you love is dying. So . . . we did something about that.

My assistant, Nadine, found us a "death doula" named Janine Violini, who deals with death much the way a birth doula deals with people being born. She loaned us so much of her grace and knowledge that the entire experience was a great one. Really. Not terrifying. Not confusing. Not overwhelming.

And so, though my mother had been slowly robbed of her memory and her health, the death that she'd never had trouble talking about was a beautiful one.

You may be thinking that starting a book about how I came into my Crone-like powers with the deaths of my parents is a little morbid. But it's an important part of this story. Their deaths turned out to be a call to arms, an awakening, even a rebirth for me.

I remember, years ago, sitting at my kitchen table looking out the window at their house across the driveway and wondering what it would be like to live on without them. I didn't think I would be able to do it. It made me anxious even to think about carrying on without their umbrella over me. Especially Mom.

But it turns out that what seems impossible is anything but that when you're dumped into it. It never ceases to amaze me how adaptable we are. We can, and do, change to cope with lives that are endlessly pushing us into new territory. My parents' illnesses and deaths taught me that I can cope with profound change. In fact, without it, I wither. Though, as I get older, I have to admit that small changes irritate me more and more—I feel like saying, "Get it over with already!" Big changes are much more manageable than the small ones.

To say it's difficult to become a person is an understatement; it takes such a long time. According to my humble estimate, it can take a human baby up to forty years to mature into a version of themselves that is of some value to the rest of society: confident, empathetic, kind, nurturing, gracious, fair, altruistic and generous. At least, that's how long it seemed to take me. A baby elephant manages to become useful to her clan in about three years, so we human beings are lagging badly behind the animal kingdom. There are grown thirty-year-olds still living in their parents' basement eating their parents' food and playing video games with another guy living in *his* parents' basement somewhere in South Korea.

I am well into my fifties now, and it's only in the last ten years that I have begun to figure out who I am. I've also figured out that, whoever I am, I'm bound to change, right up until I speed off into the netherworld. (My grandmother used to call her private parts her netherworld, but that is certainly not what I am referring to here.)

But I was talking about death, which I know most people hate talking about, except for the really old and the really young. Kids have an uncanny ability to see life and death for what it is: something that isn't static, something that is always a process. Most kids believe in some kind of heaven. They are whimsical and mystical, not yet jaded and cynical. When we die, we change from one state to another. Kids understand that with an open mind and an open heart.

As for the more experienced among us, people in their eighties or nineties often see death as a relief of sorts, a new chapter, a release, perhaps even a new beginning. I remember Mrs. Scot, our elderly neighbour from down the road, telling me one summer afternoon when I was twelve or thirteen that she couldn't wait to die so she could get her teenaged body back. She was drunk out of her mind, mind you, but still, that really made me think. When I told my mother what Mrs. Scot said, I asked if she thought it was true. "Well, that seems reasonable," she replied.

Obviously, I am still thinking about Mrs. Scot's idea of death and her idea of heaven all these decades later. I'll admit that I sometimes cringe thinking about how beautiful my body was when I was a teenager. I really couldn't see it at the time. (Why don't we see ourselves?) I might well want my old body back too. I mean, if it's an option to get it back, I'll take it! I wish I'd known back then how to appreciate my body more, to cherish it, look after it, cheer it on. But it's never too late to start doing that. I'm living proof of that.

If we don't talk about death, it becomes the monster in the closet, the hand that grabs your leg from underneath the bed. It becomes a fear that takes away from the quality of the time you have left. To live with low-grade anxiety about something you have no control over steals your happiness.

Bring death up in any conversation and watch

what happens. Hushed tones and inaudible whispers. It's actually quite funny what we do to avoid having to talk about dying.

Then there's the difficulty we often run into when we try to comfort the bereaved. We don't seem to know whether we should say something kind— which is absolutely what we should do—or avoid saying anything at all, as if bringing up the loss they suffered will somehow cause them more pain. So we let our good intentions hang awkwardly in the air because we don't want to risk hurting anybody.

But it's okay to feel hard things. It's okay to feel sad and depressed, and it's more than okay to let grief knock you off your feet. When we avoid actually feeling things, that's when life gets complicated and even more difficult than it needs to be. It's as though we've lost the tools we need to help each other. I can't believe we've become indifferent to others' suffering— the number of people who reached out to me when I wrote about feeding and caring for my mother proves otherwise—but we sure are adept at avoiding it.

"Did you hear," a typical whisper goes, "her husband died from that thing on his nose that every-body thought was a freckle . . ."

It's as if dying is a secret, a very poorly kept secret.

I am not having that. I'm going to plan my own funeral just to save my friends and family the bloody effort. I want to make it easy for everyone to say goodbye without falling apart. I am for *sure* not going to let anybody else pick the photo that goes with my obituary. People, if you can't deal with anything else, take charge of your final photograph. Honestly.

And while I'm on the subject of denial, I cannot tell you how many of my friends *do not have wills*. These are people with children and houses and businesses, and they don't have a goddamned will.

"Why don't you have a will?" I asked a colleague of mine not so long ago.

"I don't know. I guess it scares me," she said, and shrugged.

"Why? What could possibly happen to you if you got a will sorted out?"

"I don't want to think about dying. It bugs me. If I do a will, it will make it seem real—dying, that is."

Well, it *is* real. No one gets away without doing it.

Not only do I have a will, I redo it every three years. You can't imagine how many people come and go out of a will as life staggers along. I've been in several relationships over the last thirty years, none of which worked out the way I thought it would. So . . . yes, my will changes.

Because of my parents' deaths, I know how bloody complicated it can be to sort through somebody else's stuff. Especially sixty years of stuff. OH MY HELL. Just getting a dead person's phone line disconnected is ridiculous. You need a death certificate and account numbers and social insurance numbers and hair samples. (Okay, not hair samples.)

Here is just one little piece of what I went through.

ME: "Hi there, who would I talk to about having a phone line disconnected? My mom died and she won't need it anymore."

PHONE COMPANY LADY: "I'm sorry for your loss. Do you have the account number? We will need the account number and a copy of your mother's last bill faxed to us. Do you know your password?"

ME: "I'm sorry, did you say *faxed*? Also, I don't recall them having a password."

PHONE COMPANY LADY: "Yes, there is a password on this account, ma'am. Can I ask who I am speaking to? I need to verify that you have permission to access this account. And yes, ma'am, faxed. I'll transfer you now."

ME: "Transfer me to who? Hello?"

(I'm on hold for quite a while. Who chooses the music?)

NEW PHONE COMPANY LADY: "Hello, in order to disconnect the line, I need the phone number and the password attached to this account."

ME (under breath): "jesus h christ."

NEW PHONE COMPANY LADY: "Excuse me?"

ME: "I'm trying to have someone come out to disconnect my parents' home phone because they're both dead and won't be using it anymore. I don't know their password. I'm their daughter and have power of attorney, so I'm not sure what else to do here. I can give you the number I need disconnected." (I rattle off the number.)

NEW PHONE COMPANY LADY: "All right, then, I'll pull up the account. One moment. Yes, I have it here. Can I put you on hold?"

ME: "Please don't."

NEW PHONE COMPANY LADY: "I'm sorry, but I need to talk to a supervisor for this kind of transaction. One moment, please."

ME (muttering "ffs"): "Okay."

(More on-hold music comes on, and for a split second I think it's "Insensitive," but it turns out to be something else, thank God. I put the call on speakerphone because I am trying to do things—like live my life—while I am waiting. And yes, I am exaggerating, but not by much.)

NEW PHONE COMPANY LADY: "Thanks for holding. The technician will show up between March 30 and June 19, no later than noon and no earlier than 7 p.m. You need to have five pieces of ID ready for him and a small zip-lock bag of your mother's ashes."

As this book went to press, the phone had yet to be disconnected. And that was nothing compared with cancelling a dead person's credit card. I won't bore you further, but I'm still on hold for that.

As a result, when a close friend asked me recently if I would be her executor, the "No" came out of my mouth quicker than a live spider.

GET YOUR WILL SORTED OUT.

Even if you have a will, someone like me will still have to go through hell trying to disconnect your goddamned phone. But at least they'll have the power. Otherwise, it'll be a total shit show for your nearest and dearest. Even filling out one of those online wills is better than nothing.

I promise that if you get your will done, YOU WILL NOT SUDDENLY DIE. Okay, you might, but it won't be because you finally got a will.

My parents' estate was extraordinarily simple. It really was. Three kids and all the things split three ways, except for Dad's tools, which went to my older brother, Duray, because he is the only one of us who knows how to use a lathe or a band saw or a socket set or a circular sander.

Luckily for us, there was no fighting, no arguing,

no resentment of any kind. Whether the person who died owns anything at all, settling an estate can get ugly very quickly, especially when there's no will. Think of it this way: the will isn't for you but for the knuckleheads you leave behind, who will most likely fight over your $23,000 in savings, your 2009 Lexus with the dent in the door you never got around to repairing, the velvet painting of the Virgin Mary you bought on that trip to Spain and the 10k gold tennis bracelet with minuscule diamonds that every one of your children says you promised to them. Be clear. It's one last way to be kind.

Yes, good old death. Talk of it can turn any gathering into a sombre affair.

But it can actually be quite funny if you spin it right. Why do you think we have sayings like "I died laughing" or talk about "gallows humour." Laughing and dying are soulmates, I tell you.

My mother spoke about death like it was a sandwich. She was so at ease with the topic she made thinking about it mostly interesting rather than terrifying. She had many fantastic theories about what happens when you die. She told me once, for instance, that when you die, you get to see all the people who went before you in a long lineup—only in paradise they are all really nice and not all alcoholics. That made me howl.

I always wondered what happens to the people who had multiple marriages in their lives, and more than one spouse who passed away before them. Which "soulmate" do you reunite with? Mom had an answer for that too: "You pick the one you liked the best."

I hope it's that easy. I asked her what happened if that soulmate didn't pick you back? Then what? "Oh, don't be silly," she said. "Of course they'll pick you back."

Her religious leanings were broad, to say the least. When it came to explaining God to us kids, she said she had no idea who God was and that anybody who claimed to know anything about it was kidding themselves. She lamented all the fighting that went on in the world when it came to God. I'm with her on that one.

She also told us lots of whimsical childhood stories about aunts and uncles and young friends she'd lost. None of them were scary in the least, but more like wonderful fairy tales. (She had a way of turning dirt to gold.) I asked her to tell me one story in particular many times over the years. At its heart was an aunt my mother never got to meet, whose name was Anna. My grandmother Clara (my mother's mother) and Anna were two of seventeen children. Please think about that for at least a minute. Seventeen births. It was rumoured that my great-grandmother Ernestine had a couple of miscarriages as well. She was pregnant her entire adult life, and died in her mid-forties after giving birth to her last child, Winston, and suffering a massive postpartum hemorrhage.

Anyway, one fall afternoon, eight-year-old Anna was out with a few of her brothers and sisters picking crabapples to make wine and crabapple jelly. The wine was intended for my hard-drinking great-grandfather, Andrew, and the jelly for the rest of the family. Anna had an adventurous spirit and a determined disposition. And so, even though she'd been strongly cautioned by her mother not to eat too many of the tart little apples or she'd get a stomach ache, Anna gobbled dozens of them.

The following afternoon, she started to complain of stomach ache. Soon she was overcome by a crippling pain in her side, which her mother blamed on the apples. She was concerned that her little girl was in pain, of course, but she thought it would pass. Another day came and went, and it didn't pass: Anna was still in terrible pain and, by this point, also delirious. Finally they went for the doctor, who came from the nearest little town as fast as horse and buggy would carry him.

By the time he reached them, her prognosis was not good. The doctor wasn't completely sure, but he believed Anna had appendicitis. But by that point there was nothing he could do about it. Anna drifted in and out of consciousness for many agonizing hours, with her family gathered helplessly around her. Eventually, she became quiet; she seemed peaceful and pain-free. Then suddenly she sat up in her bed and pointed at the ceiling. "Can you see her? Can you see her, Mother?"

"See what?" my great-grandmother asked.

"There's an angel on the rafters."

All heads looked up at the ceiling. They didn't see anything but old wooden beams and cobwebs.

"She's right there, Mother, just behind you on the beam!"

(I would always get chills at this point in the story.)

"Oh, it's a beautiful angel come to take me home."
Right at that moment, according to my mother, Anna
took one last breath and died.

At a family reunion once, my mom took me down
to the pig barn that used to be the farmhouse where
all those children lived. It was the size of a shoebox.
The beams were still intact, including the one where
the angel had perched. I stood there and looked up
for a long time.

I like to think the story was all true. I like to think
that little eight-year-old girl really did see an angel,
and when she died, she really was going home.

I went once to visit Anna's grave in a worn-out
old cemetery in southern Alberta. I stood there in
awe. I felt such a connection to her, this relative who
had died over a hundred years ago but whom I felt
I knew from the telling and retelling of that special
story. I stood there and talked to her for a while and
left feeling inspired by the great-aunt I never knew.

When I think of my great-grandmother's
sacrifices, it makes me want to succeed in a way that
I can't completely explain. I want to do things that
she dared not even dream about. I often wonder if
she dreamed at all. I wonder if she was so saddled

with reality that dreaming only caused her pain.
I doubt she thought about herself much at all. There
were far too many things to do to spend time dreaming
of places she would never go and experiences she
could never have: she had chores to get done, meals
to prepare, children to dress and bath and teach
and raise.

Makes my head spin off. I can hardly look after
myself some days.

My mother had only a few photographs of
Ernestine. There is one, though, that she had framed.
As the old saying goes, that picture speaks a thousand
words. My great-grandmother is seated on a chair
beside her husband, who not surprisingly has a gun
propped up next to him. Some of her children are
gathered around her, all of them gazing sternly
forward. Her face is thin and determined. Her hands
are folded on her lap. Her hair is pulled back into a
tight knot. She has on a long, dark dress, most likely
the best dress she owned. Her eyes are so pale, they
must have been a beautiful blue. She looks so tired
out it actually breaks my heart.

I'm quite sure there isn't a family out there that
doesn't have a photograph exactly like this one in its

collection of distant relatives. The pioneers had one hell of a time when they got to a new place. I cannot fathom the hardships they endured, the sicknesses and the hunger and endless challenges that stood in their paths, and yet here we all are.

I keep hoping some distant cousin somewhere will come forward with a few photos I've not seen yet. One can hope. In the meantime, I treasure the one my mother framed, which now hangs on the wall in my kitchen.

2. You ask me when am I going to slow down?

I'm actually speeding up.

There isn't a single ounce of me that wants to be young(er) again. Although I wouldn't mind having my neck back. Did I already mention that? My neck has gotten shorter over the years, which is a bit odd because I feel so much *taller*. I stand in front of the mirror once in a while and pull my neck up with both hands. *Hmmmmn*, I mumble to myself as I let it fall back into its new place. At least I still have a neck, which is a good thing. I may do something about it one of these days. I have zero problems with nips and tucks or whatever it is that floats your boat, though I keep waiting for them to come up with some kind of miracle cream, something that doesn't involve a knife . . .

It's somewhat alarming for me to think back to my mid-thirties and realize how I used to navigate my politics, my morality, my ethics, my belief system, not to mention how I thought about my physical self. I'm not one of those people who don't have regrets. I regret hundreds of little things and dozens of big things. One of the big things I find myself agonizing about in the middle of the night is how much I hated my beautiful body when I was younger. And by "younger" I mean twenty to forty-nine. I only saw the light when I hit fifty. That's when I finally saw myself.

As I said earlier, why the hell do we do that to ourselves? Why can't we see how fabulous we are in the moment? Why does it take the passing of twenty years or so for us to glance at an old picture and suddenly be gobsmacked by how great we looked? Why?

One morning a few months after I'd turned fifty, I remember stopping dead in the middle of my usual routine—tweezing renegade hairs, brushing teeth, slathering on deodorant, spritzing perfume, lathering my legs with some kind of anti-cellulite lotion, slapping on makeup and blow-drying my hair. Believe you me, if I could do all of those things at the same time, I would. I was stark naked in front of the mirror—not so unusual for a person—but I guess I hadn't bothered

to LOOK at myself for a long time. I didn't really
want to see my, um—body. I still don't know what
made me stop. And don't get me wrong, I was never
one of those women who ran past a mirror dare
I catch a glimpse of myself. Not at all. I just really
never stopped to look for any length of time.
This day, I did.

Suddenly, it was as though I was staring at the
most beautiful map of the world. I saw all the places
I had been, all the things I had done, all the love, all the
strength and service my arms and legs and shoulders
and feet had given me for so many years, even though
I had put this body through such bullshit and abuse
and neglect and shame and loathing. All of that crap.
For the first time ever, I felt a shard of authentic
appreciation for this magnificent being/thing/vessel/
portal/spaceship in the mirror—and I started to cry.
I leaned on the countertop and kept looking at myself
and really got going with the tears and the snot. It
was a strange combination of embarrassment and
sadness and empathy and kindness and shame and
pride. It was super-weird and super-confusing,
because it was so many feelings happening all at
once. Eventually I had to blow my nose with a wad

of toilet paper, and then I began to laugh. I was experiencing what I can only describe as some kind of part breakdown and part breakthrough.

My five-pound dog, Midi, was none too impressed. She sat on "her" rug, looking up at me like I'd lost my marbles.

"Your human is having an episode of sorts, or sort of an episode . . ." (I talk to my dog all the time.)

"Yeah, I can see that," said Midi, whose mind I can read like I'm the Long Island Medium.

"You're a dog and you're covered in fur, and if I was covered in fur, life would have been a lot easier. I wouldn't have seen all of the unseeables."

I am pretty sure my dog thinks I am perfect just the way I am, which makes me feel good. Dogs are so non-judgmental and forgiving. Even when I've been an asshole, my dog has chalked it up to me being a human and all.

I don't know what I would do without my dog. This scruffy, grumpy little lunatic. I talk to her all day long, and I'm telling you, it has kept me sane. (It's okay: I know I'm pretty much talking to myself when I talk to her, but it's very therapeutic, so I'm going to keep right on doing it.) Midi has heard a lot about all the time I've wasted wondering if I was good enough, if I was worthy of any of the success I've had and, most of all, if I was worthy of the love in my life. I have wondered many times if I was even worthy of my friendships.

Standing in front of that mirror was a pivotal, beautiful, difficult moment that spoke so clearly to me about the truth of the cliché that it's *never* too late to appreciate and nurture and lift yourself up into a whole new life. I don't care if you're ninety-seven, it's not too late even then.

Women, especially, get to an age where they think they need to tidy things up and put things away and *slooooowwww dowwwwwwn*.

That couldn't be further from the truth. When somebody asks me when I plan on slowing down— and somebody always asks—I'm sure the look on my face is all the answer they need. Equal parts smile and scowl. Slow down? I'm actually speeding up. My body—my dear old dependable body that I didn't always appreciate—and I have a hell of a lot of things left to do.

We all do this. We look at old pictures, from a couple of years or a couple of decades ago, and we

Be yourself at all times —

wonder why we didn't "see" ourselves. We can't quite believe it was us in those photographs. It couldn't be!

"Oh my God, I WASN'T FAT AT ALL! I looked so good! My hair wasn't terrible. I had such nice arms. Look at my tiny arms! I had biceps! Look how flat my stomach was! My bum wasn't weird—it was a great bum! Why didn't I like my teeth? There was nothing wrong with my teeth! Why did I think I was so ugly? Why was I so hard on myself? Whatever happened to those jeans? I looked so good in them."

I could go on, but you get my drift. Oh, maybe just one more thing. I didn't appreciate my breasts. They were absolutely works of art. I needed a bra to *hold them down*.

For many reasons, we (meaning women mostly, when it comes to what we think about how we look) annihilate ourselves on a regular basis. And if you don't, well, good on you—you're one of the rare few who have embraced your heavenly vessel with kindness and appreciation. But most of us don't need anybody else telling us we aren't up to the mark—we're pretty good at talking ourselves down all by our lonesome. And we can't ever really know how somebody else feels about their body. I have a friend who, by all accounts, and I mean ALL accounts, has the most perfect body I've ever seen. She's strong and curvy and tall and fit and muscular and sensual and, well, the list goes on. To me, she looks completely amazing and perfect. A few years ago, during a very heartfelt late-night conversation, she told me that she hated her body, really loathed it, and was never happy with what she saw in the mirror.

I learned an invaluable lesson that evening, which was to be open and understanding to people. I've tried very hard since that night to not make assumptions about anyone. You never really know how people feel about themselves. We don't know what anyone else is going through. Our perceptions are only that, at best wild guesses as to how somebody else feels about their body or their life.

During that conversation, my friend went on to say that she wished she had a body more like mine. I was completely mind-boggled. More like mine? How was that even possible?

Thank God I had my mother. She seldom admonished me for my mistakes or my lack of belief in myself. She'd say to me, very matter-of-factly, "I don't need to tell you something you already know, Jann. You're harder on yourself than I will ever be." That always killed me to hear, especially when I was seventeen years old. I was already acutely aware of some of the bad choices I was making. She never rubbed anything in. I appreciated that more than she could have known. My mother's words of encouragement still circle around my head to this day.

For many reasons—most of which had to do with my mother—I wasn't all that hard on myself as a teenager. My mom said things to me like, "Well, you better get it out of your system, because the real world is going to disappoint you." I never quite knew what "it" was, or for that matter what indeed was the "real world."

In my twenties I had somewhat insulated myself from my foibles because I was so damn vague about everything. I was one of those people who put her head through a wall and then wondered how I got stuck there. I was the poster child for spontaneity. I didn't need to be dared to try things—I was the first person into the pool every single time. I disrupted classrooms, blurting out whatever happened to be on my mind. I was reckless and careless, and I never seemed too concerned about what might happen to me. I thrived on the unknown, the unseen and the unthinkable, and everybody around me knew that. There wasn't anything I wouldn't try, no risk I wouldn't take. I never thought about the fallout, and the results could be either thrilling or a disaster. I was learning how to be a person. I'm still that person, but I've learned to focus all that energy into being creative instead of all over the place.

What I will credit myself with, however, is the fact that I was completely and totally "in the moment." There was no future and no past. As far as I was concerned, I hadn't lived long enough to have a past. Perhaps you'd call that carefree or naive—or put it down to the fact that I was a late bloomer. My mom told me I was a late bloomer right up to the end of her life, which always made me laugh. Maybe it was her way of calling me aloof? I was fifty-six when she died. All I know is that I was that person who was trying to live their entire life in one day. I always opted for instant gratification. I no more wanted to wait for things to happen than to pull out my own teeth. I wanted to feel everything exactly right then and there.

And yes, it is possible to bloom extremely late in life. I am blooming as I sit here. I can feel myself blooming. You can never stop blooming, people. That's the best part of being a human being.

3. Being an adult has its disadvantages.

I don't think I became a person—meaning a somewhat capable, self-conscious, empathetic, thoughtful, kind and relatively intelligent human being—until I was forty-five years old. Growing up for me actually meant allowing some childlike qualities back into my life. After a couple of decades of trying to be an adult, I was pretty damn serious and tortured about everything. I much preferred the bull-running-around-the-china-shop version of myself, to be honest. For a long while I turfed really useful qualities such as playfulness and creativity and using one's imagination in favour of responsibility and seriousness and maturity, for God's sake, none of which I found to be too helpful.

For whatever reason, as we leave our teens and twenties, a stick starts ever so slowly to work its way

up our arse. We get into some sort of groove.
Maybe more of a habit than a groove. We abandon
our instincts and start doing more and more things
that we think we *should* be doing. The need to be
practical and diligent and sensible is jammed into
our heads on a constant basis. That's the only way
to be successful and happy, people tell us. That's
what it is to be grown-up. You have to be in control
of your life. You have to have good habits. My dad
used to call a habit "a bad idea running around
a burning house with a can of gasoline." I sort of
get what he meant, and it certainly is a visual: you
know something is bad for you, but you do it anyway.
We do a lot of things that make us unhappy as we get
older, and we keep doing them because we don't
know how to stop.

I always felt I needed to do what other people
thought I should be doing. I was so worried about
other people's perception of me that I kept forgetting
what I wanted, thinking I better not let anybody
down or else. The funny part was that I was letting
myself down, constantly.

We become afraid of succeeding on our own
terms, which is so nutty. We're afraid of our own

greatness. It's easier than you think to get distracted from living your own life.

A friend of mine was always telling me that it was of paramount importance to know what was going on in the world; knowing what was going on would make me look good in the eyes of important, smart, successful people. This was a person I greatly admired and who had a lot of influence on me.

I was never really all that interested in tuning in to the twenty-four-hour news cycle. I did not find it empowering in the least, but rather deflating on many levels. But I admired my friend, and so I tried as hard as I could to follow her advice. I watched the damned news and did my best to act enthusiastic. It didn't last.

I finally reassured myself that it was okay not to know all the hideous things going on in the world at every single moment. If the important, smart people were going to think less of me for tuning out world events, so be it. I can't believe I felt such pressure from my friend that I tried to change who I was. I'm using this as an example to show we don't usually see the obvious. We end up doing things we don't want to do because we want to please the people around us.

To this day, I still feel this strong desire to bolt out of bed and turn on the news to find out what's happened in the world while I slept—even though I know that being aware of every shitty thing that's going on in the world seriously affects my ability to be happy. It's as simple as that. By this I don't mean that I've lost interest in this big old world of ours, just that I can't be monitoring it all day long, because that makes me feel sick.

My mom said that when she was growing up, they never knew what was going on at the farm next door, let alone what was happening across an ocean. And as much as I thought that must have been odd, I also thought what a blessing it might have been not to know the exact nature of the turmoil in the world.

When someone brings up the latest news to me these days, be it at the grocery store or a dinner party or a coffee shop, saying, "Did you hear about the blankety blank blank . . ." I am content to reply, "No, I didn't hear. I haven't really been watching the news."

"It was terrible—you should have seen it." People love spreading bad news. I wish that wasn't true, but it is. I think it has something to do with facing our own mortality. When bad things happen to other people, we breathe a collective sigh of relief that it didn't happen to us, and we want to talk about it.

"I can imagine." I try to sound interested.

"It was absolutely horrible."

"Well, have a good day," I say, and nod goodbye.

Ten years ago, such an encounter would have left me feeling stupid and uninformed—out of sync with reality somehow. Now I know that I can't take it all on, not because I don't care, but because it can be paralyzing. My mom always used to tell me that I'd hear about the "big things" through the grapevine. (I think the grapevine turned into the Internet.) "The big things find you no matter where you are," she'd say as she wiped off a countertop. Mom never stopped cleaning—ever. Yes, I suppose the big things will find you no matter where you are. "If someone lost an arm in a threshing machine, you'd hear about it," she'd say with a laugh. "That would have been big news and someone would have driven down to tell us about it. It's not like we didn't know there was a war going on, Jann. We would always know about the big things."

I was standing at a baggage claim a few weeks ago that featured a giant screen blasting one of the big news outlets. I tried not to pay attention to it, but there

I stood, a captive audience, waiting for my very beat-up, red Briggs & Riley bag to appear on the carousel, staring at that TV along with everybody else. There had been yet another mass shooting somewhere and another conflict was happening halfway around the world—the usual absurdity of politics and terror attacks—and then came a quick splash of an "uplifting" story about a kid running a lemonade stand to raise money to help clean the plastic out of the ocean. By the time I picked up my bag, I'd had a full report on the globe. Why airports think it's a good idea to subject jet-lagged people to that, I'll never know.

Since the big things find you no matter where you are, it's okay to unhook from your portable news source so you're not in the middle of what's happening every minute of the day. It doesn't mean you don't care; it means you care about yourself too.

A weird sidebar on the news, since I seem to be talking about dying on and off throughout this book: An old friend of mine works at one of Canada's major networks and she told me that they—meaning the network—have a bunch of footage ready to air in case I was to, well, suddenly die.

I'm sure she saw the look of shock on my face. I could feel my forehead turning into an accordion.

She quickly clarified: "Not just for you. We have footage for a lot of public people."

"Like, the news story is all ready to go in case I die? I hope they don't show Live 8 concert footage from back in July 2005, because I was super-fat at that thing." I said that to her. Those words actually came tumbling out of my mouth, though I would be dead and it would not matter to me in the least.

"I don't know what they have on the reel, but yes, they're ready just in case you drop dead."

We both laughed, but she laughed a little harder and longer than I did.

When I think back to who I was thirty-five years ago, I'm amazed that I'm still alive to write this. I was absolutely out of control. I drank too much and thought too little. I spent much of my time in triage mode, trying to deal with an enormous amount of guilt over the way I was living my life, nursing hangovers or worrying my stupid fool head off that I was pregnant. The drinking made me lose all sense of inhibition, and the lack of inhibition made me unbelievably promiscuous. I was trying to figure out who I was and what made me tick, although being drunk was the worst possible way of figuring anything out.

I regret it all, I still do, but I've been able to sift through it and make good use of those troubled times.

Even in the midst of all that mess, I had a weird sense that things would be okay. No matter what I did to myself, no matter how low I got, how desperate or how broke, I was convinced I would somehow survive. I kept telling myself that the best was yet to come and hoped I wasn't lying to myself.

I had a partner, many years ago, who told me she couldn't deal with my optimism. That stayed with me for years. She didn't like my optimism? My optimism has always been the thing I like the most about myself. It's like having sunlight in your pocket on a dark day. I think I eventually succeeded because of it.

Optimism is the thing that can carry you out of a fire. When you *think* you can do something, at least you have a shot at getting it done. When you think you can't, you won't. I'm not trying to be all preachy preacherson here, but you know that's true. Thoughts are tangible things. Intentions are valuable, and the intentions you have for yourself and your future can make all the difference in the world.

Good things come out of bad things. I'm going to keep telling you that.

Let's face it, judging yourself takes time out of your already busy day. It takes effort to rake yourself over the coals and diminish your spirit. You have to stop whatever it is you're doing and say horrible things to yourself about your legs or your arms or your lips or your chin or your toes or your knees or your earlobes or your eyelashes or your nostrils or your fingers or your wrists or your ankles or your brain or your heart.

When we're young (especially for women), there is no end to what we don't like about ourselves. I was constantly comparing myself with other people, and those very same people were comparing themselves with *me*. That is a fact. My mother used to say, "One man's ceiling is another man's floor," and my dad used to say, "One man's tragedy is another man's triumph." You can see what I was dealing with here. These two came at life from very different angles. My dad also used to say, "Don't be careful, be sorry." I never liked that one. Maybe he was trying to be funny, but it wasn't.

Good

come

Bad

things

out of

things

When I was younger, I felt as though I spent most of my time just processing: trying to figure out how to be a decent person. I was trying to like myself, and of course I was hoping that other people would like me too. We all want to be liked. I often felt stuck between being too self-aware and not being self-aware enough. I'm so relieved there was no Internet back then. I am so happy that most of the really stupid things I did in the seventies and eighties aren't trapped for an eternity on the World Wide Web—things like peeing in a garbage can at a country and western bar (there was a really long lineup for the women's washroom) or barfing up pizza and beer off the thirty-seventh floor of a hotel. The thirty-seventh floor! Can you even?

I did a lot of things that I am not proud of and that I'm ashamed of, but my God, I've learned from them, and I'm still learning.

The Internet has profoundly changed the judgment climate—not only how we judge ourselves, but how we judge others. The negative impact on the lives of young women all over the globe is alarming, sad and dangerous. I hate to say this, but it feels as if it is here to stay. Any of us who grew up in a time when social media had not yet been conjured up from the depths of hell—okay, that's a titch dramatic, but you know what I mean—will realize this.

The world was a different place before social media got invented. Online bullying is ending lives. What's happening online to my friends' teenaged daughters is beyond frightening—a culture of shaming and bullying that has somehow been so normalized. It doesn't feel good, that's for sure. I don't know how I would handle being fourteen or fifteen in today's climate. I really don't have a clue. I have a difficult time with social media at fifty-seven, so I can't fathom how the kids are dealing with it. I thought the old-fashioned bullying that happened on the school grounds at recess, a taunt or a jab that came from someone right in front of you, was bad, but it had nothing on what goes on now. At least you could see your bully back then. Call it *knowing your enemy* if you will, but you could see their face. When you don't know who the enemy is because of the anonymity of the Web, it could be anyone and everyone—a bunch of punches thrown at you in the pitch dark from every direction. That's what it feels like. Anonymous comments

and anonymous insults from anonymous places
and anonymous people.

Some people would disagree with me on this,
but I block people immediately. I don't offer any
second chances—I block people at the first indication
of trouble. They are *my* social media feeds, after all,
be it Twitter or Facebook or whatever. If there's
negativity or disparaging remarks, I block.

Don't get me wrong. Social media can have
profound positive aspects too, bringing awareness
to myriad issues in a way that couldn't be done even five
or ten years ago. It's a place to tell our stories, to garner
support, to start a group or a forum for people to share
their concerns and worries and problems, to start a
movement. The Internet can be a place of learning and
discovery: think of the way it has shaped the audio and
visual arts. Yep, the Internet knocked the knees out
from under the music industry, disrupting the hell out
of the business model. But I can record a song and
make it available in a hundred countries the next day
with one click. The Internet's usefulness is entirely
powered by the person using it.

We can dive into other people's moment-to-
moment lives these days, and that can be both good

and bad. To the good: Amber Alerts when a child goes missing, mobilizing a whole community, even a whole country.

We can track each other using our cellphones, which is both awesome and creepy. I actually don't want anybody to know where I am—unless I'm stranded in the desert without an ice-cold drink and air conditioning. In that case, please feel free to track me down using satellites hurtling through space. Other than that, no, I don't think so. I don't ever tag my photos. Yes, I tweet fairly frequently, but I don't want anybody to know exactly what I'm up to twenty-four hours a day. I certainly don't want anyone to know that I am at HomeSense again.

Say what you will, the Internet and all its complexities are here to stay, user beware. It can be a difficult thing to navigate. But you don't have to be a victim, nor do you need to tolerate any form of bullying or cruelty. Block, report, repeat. Mean people suck, but mean people are hurt people; I often remind myself of that when someone is gunning for me. I wonder to myself what in the heck made them so awful, and I honestly try to be as empathetic and as understanding as I possibly can.

I still block, though, because nobody needs to take shit from anybody. I'm a lot of things, but I'm not mean. Rather than fire back, I consider blocking someone, simply bowing out.

4. When pants fly.

In my twenties, I was scattered and disorganized.
I didn't often think things through, because I was
scared and uncertain. Scattered and disorganized
very often result from scared and uncertain, don't
you think?

I flew by the seat of my pants, but I felt like
that's what we were all doing—or maybe I needed
to believe that everyone was as unorganized as me.
(They weren't, as it turns out. Most of my friends
were diligent and determined and on the ball.) I had
barely graduated from high school and, before I knew
what hit me, I was half-lit in some dingy, sticky, dark
little bar, singing cover songs and eating french fries
and sleeping with guys whose names I very seldom
knew. It was not pretty.

Back then, all I wanted to possess was some kind of wisdom. I wanted to be sure of *something*. I wanted to know who I was and I wanted someone other than my mother to tell me I was going to be okay. Little did I know that I was going to have to become the person who would tell me I was going to be all right. Though you can't skip ahead in life, some part of me knew I had to power through, and so that's what I did.

Most of my high school friends had colleges lined up or had planned for a gap year that included ten months of backpacking through Europe or had jobs waiting for them with the family business. My dad had a concrete business, but I could not see myself doing that. I did work for him the summer I was fifteen, and he said to me, "You were the worst goddamned employee I ever had." (I hated that job more than you could possibly know. I laid something called rebar into wooden forms—long steel bars that reinforced the poured concrete. I *was* a terrible employee. I spent most of my time drinking bad coffee out of a Thermos and eating cheese balls.)

When I graduated, I didn't have a single plan, which may well have contributed to my fear. At the time, self-realization was not my thing. I lived in the blur of denial, envying the planners, who seemed to have it all figured out.

I didn't plan on *not* being a planner. I thought I should actually *be* a planner. After all, we are told our whole lives that we need a plan—that we HAVE to have a plan. "What's the plan, Jann?"

On several occasions, I remember I did sit down with a pencil in hand (easily erasable) and made columns and jotted things madly, and after a half hour or so I realized I was staring out the window, thinking about what I should eat.

At eighteen, my list looked something like this:

—Get a decent-paying job (how?)
—Move out of Mom and Dad's (need a job to do so)
—Pay parking tickets (see previous point)
—Figure out life (get a decent-paying job)
—Buy some Howick jeans (sure, that'll help)
—See ABBA in concert (I can get behind this one, a hundred percent)

Not a plan at all. More like a cry for help.

God knows, my parents were desperate for me to

have a plan. They didn't care what the plan entailed, just that I had one.

But what about those of us who aren't planners? What about *us*? I'm telling you, this planning business is not the only way forward. Life for the most part happens whether you have a plan or not.

That doesn't mean you're not prepared. Even at my worst, I was ready and willing to deal with anything that came my way. That's a good thing, right? I wasn't precious about any of it. If unsavoury things happened to me, I dealt with them to the best of my ability and tried not to feel sorry for myself. That was something I learned from my dad. Obstacles were my thing. I expected to fail, and I didn't think that a failure was the end of the world.

It may sound way too simple, but I think my goal was to try to be happy. No matter what I ended up doing, or being, I knew I wanted to be happy. That's no small thing.

My parents always told me that I had better plan on having the kind of job where I didn't have to work for anybody. "Jann, I don't know who is going to hire you." Both of them said that. My mom was always worried about what I was going to do with my life.

Looking back, I don't blame her one bit. Every parent worries about their children, and I was so glad that somebody worried about me. My folks weren't perfect by any stretch of the imagination, but I knew they loved me. I knew that because, when they caught me doing things I shouldn't have been doing, I always got in big trouble.

I knew kids in school whose parents didn't care where they went or what they did, and they were all kinds of screwed-up and insecure. I remember this rich kid named John who prided himself on skipping most of his classes and selling hash oil just because he could. "My parents don't give two shits what I do," he said to me on more than one occasion. Not one, but *two* shits. At the time, I thought, "Wow, that's super-cool that you get to do whatever you want and nobody gives, well, two shits."

I think back now to how lonely that must have been for him. We all want someone to care where we are and whom we're with and what time we're going to be home. We think we don't, but we do. I would take strict parenting over no parenting any day.

When I was about fifteen, my mom actually marched into the middle of a party my friend Shelly

Hambrooke was throwing on a school night because her parents were away. I don't know how Mom even knew there *was* a party at Shelly Hambrooke's, but she did. There were boys there and probably beer— I can't remember all the details. But I do have a vivid recollection of the music seeming to stop as my mother carved her way through the teenage angst and grabbed the collar of my jean jacket and hauled me out to her car. I'd lied to her, I remember that. I'd told her I was going somewhere else. I was ashamed at the time, but remembering that awkward moment now fills me with love. She gave two shits about me, always, and I'm so grateful.

So I wasn't a planner, but I've always felt this hand on my shoulder adjusting my direction. Sometimes it was my mother's, for sure, but sometimes it was the universe. I'm not particularly religious, but I believe wholeheartedly that there's an observant presence around us. I guess I could say God. I don't mind saying God. I simply don't believe in a guy sitting on a giant white marble throne handing out punishments like a petulant four-year-old.

But, all right, I will say I believe in God going forward, because I do believe in God—I'm just not completely sure of what that is. But I'm working on it. Sorry that sounded so confusing. I didn't mean it to be. I'm always a bit jealous of people who seem to know exactly what and whom they believe in. I believe in spirituality, I really do, and I also believe in science.

This little story has always stuck with me (I forget who told it to me—I wish I could give them the credit): So there's a theologian, a priest, a shaman, a rabbi, what have you, and a scientist climbing up different sides of the same mountain. They almost kill themselves getting to the top, and when they finally do, they stare at each other in disbelief. They each felt that their "truth" was the only "truth," and I suppose they were very surprised to see one another.

I feel that science is in the mix somewhere when it comes to religion for me. I guess, at the end of the day, we all want to believe in something good, and I do for sure believe in something good.

It's taken me decades to appreciate how important and pivotal the obstacles and hardships I've encountered have been to my life. The *only* reason I ended up being a singer-songwriter is that my dad was an alcoholic. He was one of those guys who had one drink and instantly sought out an argument or someone to pick on.

It's hard for me to say these next words out loud, because they make me feel ashamed: my dad was a textbook bully. As a child, I spent an inordinate amount of time at my friends' houses in order to stay out of his way. Since we lived in the country, it was fairly easy to grab a different school bus after the last bell rang and get dropped a few acreages away, at somebody else's house. My mother actually encouraged it. I remember her saying, "Don't bring any kids home after school, because you don't know what your dad is going to be like."

My dad was unpredictable. I never knew whether he was going to be the drunk dad who handed me five bucks and told me a joke or the drunk dad who grabbed my older brother's ear and twisted it while he cried, "Please don't, Dad!"

In either scenario, Dad thought he was being super-hilarious.

My mom did everything she could to protect my two brothers and me, but you can't keep all of the abuse and the fear and the confusion away forever; it seeps in through the cracks. Then there was the weird fact that everyone—including my dad—was in complete denial that anything was wrong. It's amazing what "normal" can be: a hideous fog that gets thicker as every year staggers past. It's taken me decades to realize how dysfunctional our family was, but I do not regret that dysfunction. Every single shitty event led me to where I am today.

Good things come out of bad things. Had my father not been an alcoholic, I wouldn't have found myself in the basement. I think about that a lot. I wouldn't have gone down there. I wouldn't have played records or learned to play the guitar. It wouldn't have happened.

As I grew older, my dad came home later and later from his job. His drinking got worse. It took over his whole life. When the back door finally flew open at whatever hour of the day or night and my dad staggered in, I would make sure I was down in our dingy basement. My parents fixed it up over the years with new lights and some fake bricks slapped over the grey concrete, but it remained very much a basement, with no windows, and it had a constant dampness that made your bones cold. Since nobody in their right mind voluntarily wanted to spend time down there, it was a perfect place to hide from my drunk dad.

Luckily for me, the record player was down there as a bonus, along with hundreds of LPs that provided me with endless entertainment. Who knew I'd pick up my mom's old guitar, propped in the corner like a broomstick, and change my entire life's trajectory. I didn't plan on that happening. No planning whatsoever. Good things come out of bad things.

Something that began for me out of fear and avoidance changed my life. You don't get to know until much later how these things work. Do I look back and wish I'd known, when I was plucking away hour after hour on that guitar, that my path in life would burst open because of it? Probably not. I have no desire, even now, to know the future.

My friend Nigel, whom I have known for almost twenty years, has often pointed out that the only part of the future he wants to know is what he is going to eat next. It's kind of hilarious, because it's true. Whenever I go on holiday with him, or visit him in the UK, we're planning lunch right after we've had breakfast, and right after we have lunch, we're planning dinner. I think planning the next meal is the centre of every relationship. If you can find another human who wants to eat with you for the rest of your life, you're set. I wonder if there is an app for that.

The last thing that ever crossed my young mind was that I would become a musician of any description. People who looked like me did not become professional singers. But over the next twenty years, each of the many times I tried to distance myself from singing or writing or performing, I was dragged back by some mysterious force. I didn't plan one damn thing. I wasn't a planner and I never have been. Okay, now I'll stop talking about planning.

The biggest surprise to me was that I didn't even know I liked music until I started hiding from my dad in the basement. It had been there in the background of my life, pouring out of a radio some-where, but I never thought about it much. Spinning the old records for hours in the basement changed that. I became obsessed with learning the songs I listened to, singing and playing along, and soon began making up my own. If Dad hadn't been drunk all the time, it never would have happened. I didn't even like going down to the basement to retrieve a loaf of bread out of the freezer. Before they upgraded the fixtures, the place was lit by a single bulb screwed into the ceiling, which had a string dangling from it that you had to yank to turn the light on. I hated throwing my arms around madly in the dark to find that string—it was always unnerving.

I would never have dreamed back then that I would feel as passionate about anything as I do about music. My maternal grandmother, Clara, said that the best-laid plans were designed by fate and misfortune. I love that saying. So many extraordinary things have been born from hardship and disaster. Such great music and literature and art and poetry. I'm grateful for my own obstacles, that's for sure.

I didn't know how bad my dad's alcoholism was until I saw him sober. At times he'd sit reading a pocket book in his chair, drinking coffee and puffing away on a cigarette and ignoring us completely. He put out a force field that made it clear he wanted to be left alone. We didn't dare disturb him or even stay in the same room. All these years later, I understand that those were the times he was recovering from being on a bender. Eventually, I was able to see the broken, unsure man who drank to cover up all the doubt. It was heartbreaking.

For a lot of his drinking years, I was too young to conceptualize what was happening to him, let alone have the tools to cope. Maybe he didn't have the tools either. He was a human being, but I didn't see that, I only saw Dad—the version I couldn't count on. I am constantly working on finding kindness in my heart for him, or, if not kindness, a sliver of redemption. He was doing his best, I suppose, to bring home a paycheque and tame his demons. When you are a child, parents are cooks, cleaners, doctors, referees, teachers, therapists, drivers, coaches, preachers, gods and monsters. They are not human beings.

Good things come out of bad things.

I regret not taking more time to unravel the mystery that was my father while he was alive. I wish I had been able to ask him things about himself without feeling awkward and still slightly fearful. I wish I could have offered him more grace and forgiveness, but, at times at least, I hated him. He was hard to like and even harder to love, let's put it that way.

I'm riddled with regrets—the piercing kind that shoot through your head on a quiet Sunday afternoon and hurt your eyebrows. They almost always spring from my use of alcohol (the irony is not lost on me) and include nudity and harsh words and thoughtless, unkind actions—especially towards myself. In my fifties, I still get these unpredictable pangs of remorse. Sometimes I can laugh a little about the things I did, but more often I cringe and shake my head.

I was hiking with a friend a few months ago when I had a wildly random regret recollection that fired through my torso like a bad meal. I drew a sharp breath through my teeth.

My friend stopped on the dirt trail and grabbed my arm. "What the hell, Jann?"

"I'm okay. I just had a fucking weird regret fly through me." I took a slug of water from my stainless steel bottle.

"Jesus, I thought something bit you."

I laughed. "It kind of did."

"Is that normal for you?"

"Come on, don't you ever get those?" I said. "Things you buried for so long you almost forgot, and then wham!" We started walking again.

"Regrets are stupid," she said in a way that made me want to whack her in the arm—the sign of a true friendship.

"Really? Regrets aren't that stupid, are they? They're reminders of how far you've come. They're reminders that you've tried to expand yourself."

"What's in that water?" she said, then laughed and proceeded to tell me that I was being too hard on myself and that I was a big weirdo. "I seriously thought something bit you."

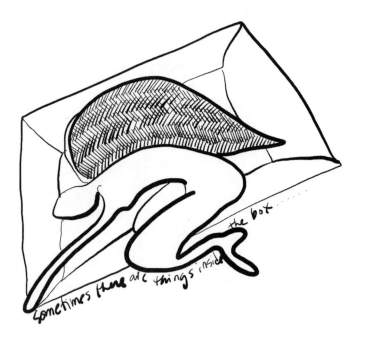

sometimes there are things inside the box . . . . . .

5. The upside of falling down.

Show me someone who hasn't failed and I'll show you someone who hasn't tried. Didn't Kermit the Frog say that? Or the Dalai Lama? Or was it Madonna? One of those people. My dad offered up a slightly different version: "If you're not failing, you're not trying." He wasn't wrong. My dad may have been an alcoholic, but he was the hardest-working alcoholic I've ever known other than Elizabeth Taylor—although I didn't know her.

My dad was never not trying and, thusly, never not failing. Although he never let on, his concrete business was always in peril. But he didn't throw in the towel—although I'm sure he wanted to a hundred times—he just kept trying new ways to keep going forward. I admired him for that, and I told him as

If you're

that means

smiling —

you're

trying !

much when both of us were older. No one worked harder than my father. Watching him drag himself, half-drunk, out to his truck every morning and head down our little road to work left a lasting impression on me that is reflected in my own work ethic. But he didn't know how to enjoy himself without alcohol. Alcohol was both his punishment and his reward, and I can relate to that big time.

He had gotten it into his head that life was hard, goddamn it, and you just had to mop your brow, set your jaw and stiffen your upper lip and push through. He was such a serious guy. Maybe watching him all those years—seeing that brooding, miserable demeanour at our dinner table night after night, if he even made it home for dinner—made me want to spread sweetness and light. Still, I'm a lot like my dad. Trust me, I fight it. I share his temper and his pouting and his anger and his cynicism. I can let all those things fly if I let my guard down.

Good things come out of bad things.

For me, failing, in the moment that it's happening, is completely horrible and exhausting. I hate it, I really do, and I'm pretty sure everyone else does too. I have learned, though, as time goes by, that each failure always reveals itself to be an instance where Merlin steps out of the mist with his long staff and saves the day. It's never as bad as you think it's going to be. There's always something positive that comes of it, though you might not see that right away. You might not realize that Merlin was there saving you until decades later. Failing is a necessity, I'm afraid, especially if you want to get anywhere.

I have failed at so many things, it's impressive. I don't have any regrets in that department. I am no more afraid of failing than I am of succeeding. Most of us are unbelievably afraid of succeeding, because succeeding can be as nerve-racking as losing out. There have been studies done on how human beings cope with good things happening to them. Not surprisingly, we generally expect not to get what we want. Nobody actually thinks they'll win the lottery, so when they do, all hell breaks loose.

There is a tiny voice in my head that always says in any crisis, "Keep going." Maybe it's the lasting effect of my mother's eternally positive nature on my heart. I don't know. But that voice is a persistent one, and it's been getting louder as the years wear on. Maybe it's the Crone in me, finding her way out of the trees . . .

As I have gotten older, failure means something entirely different to me. Failure feels entirely different too. It isn't a negative thing at all. It feels productive and worthwhile.

I think, as young women, we internalize not getting what we want. We decide it isn't happening because we aren't smart enough or pretty enough or tall enough or thin enough. We convince ourselves that we aren't as valuable as the person who wins the prize. The little voice in our head becomes a cacophony of confusing and misleading information. Why is it so easy to believe the negative stuff and so difficult to accept the positive and the magnificent?

I was lucky to have a mother who on a regular basis said things like "Jann, why *not* you? You're just as good as anybody." I don't think she understood the impact her words had on me. My mother's encouragement and my dad's absence made for an interesting cocktail. It turns out that her tenderness and his ferociousness both had equal value.

Neither of my parents—not the tender one nor the scary one—stepped in to fight my battles, fix my troubles or remove my obstacles. On that score, they were a solid front. If I got myself into trouble, I had to get myself out of it. If, let's say, I burned down part of the neighbour's fence or seized the engine of my 1976 Ford Pinto because I forgot to put oil in it, I was the one who had to pay to fix those things.

"Don't you know what a goddamned oil light means when it's lit up for a goddamned month, Jann?"

I thought it was something to do with the seat belts?

My dad was so mad over that one. He had to bring his truck up the road to where my car died to tow me home. I can still picture him lying underneath the front bumper, trying to tie a thick yellow rope around something that would hold when he towed me. He swore the whole time. When he swore, rainbows appeared in the sky, rockets shot to the moon, the ground rumbled—it was that impressive a display. I think his swearing kept him alive an extra ten years, especially after he got sober, given that he swore even more. Remembering some of the swear combinations he came up with still makes me laugh. The F-word was saved for very serious situations. People who swear literally do live longer. That's science, people.

My parents didn't have a lot of money to dole out, so I had a part-time job at the nearby golf course by the time I was thirteen. I wanted my own money,

and it made me feel very accomplished when I got
a cheque for a whopping thirty bucks after two weeks
of cleaning golf clubs.

So many parents seem to think that removing the
hard things from their children's way is going to keep
them from harm. I think it causes more harm, more
difficulty, more confusion. If you don't learn about
problem solving at a young age, you can't expect to
effectively navigate problems in adulthood. I mean,
it's one thing to stop a kid from falling off a ledge at
the Grand Canyon and another to refuse to let them
play in a bouncy ball pit because there might be
flesh-eating bacteria in amongst the balls. Isn't
there always?

Life is full of peril, but you've got to live it none-
theless, flesh-eating disease be damned. I jumped in
a bouncy ball house about five years ago at my friend's
son's bar mitzvah, and it was super-fun until I found
half of a grilled cheese sandwich. No, I did not eat it. In
fact, I did not even touch it. I left it there for the other
bouncers. I do recall saying to somebody bouncing
next to me, "Hey, I think I just saw a grilled cheese
sandwich." They didn't seem too concerned. (The bar
mitzvah had an open bar, so I think that helped.)

I had a sort of friend, years ago, who had two young children, preteen girls about nine and eleven, I think. I'm terrible at guessing ages, but that's what I'm going to go with. I know for sure they weren't in their forties. Their mother invited me for coffee one afternoon to pick my brain about a project she'd been working on for her church. Trust me, I wanted to decline, but she was determined. When I got to her house, she had what I thought was her own project spread out on her giant dining room table. There was what looked like a papier mâché volcano and a miniature town with trees and cars and little houses with furniture. I was like, "Wow, Marlene!" (Her name is NOT Marlene.) "This looks crazy great. What is your project for?"

"Oh, no, this is my daughter's homework assignment. She needs to have it handed in by Thursday."

"You're doing your daughter's homework?" I wanted to run out of the house or call the cops or eat a giant bag of salt-and-vinegar chips. I think my eyes got really big and filled with visible alarm.

"OMG, yeah! All the parents at the school help with their kids' stuff. It's kind of a known thing. The teachers totally get it."

I don't remember what Marlene's actual church project was about. I was so distracted by the fact that she was doing her kid's homework that I've blanked it. My parents would no more have done my homework for me than performed an appendectomy on the family dog. My mother once tried an at-home perm on me after I begged her, and that was a disaster. That perm took seven years to completely grow out.

I remember feeling sorry for Marlene's kids. Here was a parent thinking she was doing her daughter some giant favour by making this school project look absolutely perfect, and all she was doing was squashing her creativity and stifling her imagination. Making things is what childhood is all about. Making things is what life is all about. Making things for yourself is the most glorious damn thing on the planet. You can even make money making things.

I make stuff for a living. It's fantastic. I literally *make up songs* and people pay me. I am beyond grateful and astonished every waking minute of my day.

I've seen Marlene once or twice since then at different functions around town. I always regret not telling her that she shouldn't have been doing her kid's homework. I completely understand that it's not any of my business. I don't think it would have gone over well if I had said anything. But it still bugs me that I didn't just tell her that *helping* with your kid's homework and *doing* your kid's homework are two very different things.

So I'm saying it now: If you're doing your kid's homework, stop it. Let your kid do their own damn homework, and if it's not perfect, well, so what. And, yes, they might even fail and the volcano might end up looking like a molehill. They can handle that— succeeding or failing on their own. It's going to make them awesome, steadfast, confident humans.

As a side note, I've never had kids, but I was one. My parents' idea of helping me with my homework was making me sit at the kitchen table until it was done—without food or water. Okay, I had milk. But we got our milk from a farmer down the road who had actual cows, and it was very thick and not the easiest stuff in the world to swallow. It actually made me gag. My mother would tell me I was being dramatic, which I was. She brought the milk home in a giant steel canister, and it had four inches of cream on top of it that we had to strain off with a piece of cheesecloth. (Cheesecloth is not made of cheese.) I don't drink milk anymore and I think having to do my homework at the kitchen table with a glass of milk sitting in front of me for hours is the reason.

Back to the main point: failing has been crucial to building my resilience in life. I don't think I've ever learned a whole hell of a lot from getting it right—from experiencing success. It was all the crap I went through before I got anywhere that seems important to me now. I pull strength from the hardships, not the triumphs. Triumphs are great and all, but they are like false prophets: if you follow their lead, you end up scared that you'll never be that "good" again, and you shut yourself down. I was rejected by every record company on the planet, several times in fact. I have rejection letters that are epic. I've saved them all, and occasionally I'll pull them out and read them to remind myself that those rejection letters were actually love notes cheering me on. Criticism says more about the person handing it out than the person on the receiving end. I would rather be the creative person who wrote a bad song than the critic calling it a bad song.

The author of one letter told me that my songs were "too personal." I remember reading that line over and over, and thinking, "Aren't songs supposed to be personal?" I mean, what's the point otherwise? Should I have been writing "impersonal" songs? If so, what did one of those sound like?

At the time, I felt blindsided by the negativity. Here was a complete stranger—someone who didn't know me from a papier mâché volcano—telling me that my songs were too personal. I should drag that letter out right now and google the ass off that guy. He's probably running a pyramid scheme somewhere. One of the big lessons for me here was: *It doesn't matter what anybody else thinks. What matters is what you think.*

Despite the rejections, it never occurred to me to change what I was writing, because I loved what I was doing so much. I loved how the music made me feel and I loved that in my songs I was being completely honest. I didn't want to change a thing. Yes, I wanted to get better—be a better writer, be a more seasoned, experienced vocalist—but I knew that both of those things required time and persistence. I have told many an aspiring singer-songwriter that persistence is almost always going to trump talent. Talent without persistence isn't going to get you anywhere. Determination can persuade anyone who is sitting on the fence to side with you.

Talent is subjective in every form of art. Yes, there are rare exceptions. Mozart comes to mind, because he was *Mozart*. But for the most part, if you show ten people a painting or play them a song, they will all have a different opinion about it. If I'd listened to the advice in every one of my rejection letters, I would have ended up sounding like anything but me.

As the years have worn on, I have realized that being myself is my most important, most valuable tool. I have made a living being myself. Being envious of other people's talents will make you bitter. Being envious of other people will steal your joy. Be yourself. Believe me, the sooner you are able to cheer yourself on, the better. Do what YOU do and BE who YOU are.

The last Hail Mary attempt my first manager, Neil, and I made to get me a record deal is one of those stories that continually make me shake my head in wonderment. The short version of it is this: We had sent a cassette of ten acoustic songs to a man named

Allan Reid at A&M Records in Toronto. Allan's name had been given to us by a man named Doug Chappell, who had turned us down the previous week. Allan was twenty-six years old, tall, handsome, new to his job at the label, which was to find and sign exciting new acts that would hopefully make everybody some money. No pressure . . .

At that time, in the early nineties, grunge was the thing every label was chasing. Nirvana had hit hard, along with Pearl Jam, Soundgarden and the Stone Temple Pilots, to name a few. It was like a male-dominated landslide racing towards us from the west coast of the United States, engulfing us all. That's what all the labels were looking for. Not someone like me. I was the furthest thing from grunge.

Allan received the cassette (in the mail, because what else was there?) and told Neil that he would listen and get back to us ASAP. My hopes weren't high. As I said, I had rejection letters and phone calls coming out my yin-yang, so I was feeling fairly vulnerable.

Allan plugged the tape into the deck of his car, because who doesn't love to play music in their car, and he listened in earnest because he really wanted to like it. The songs were mostly ballads, the arrangements simple, stripped down, just me and my guitar. Most of them leaning to the depressing side of things, if I'm honest.

It wasn't a complete surprise when Allan passed. He told Neil that I was good, but that he didn't have a clue what the label could do with me, or where my music fit in as far as the "climate" of the industry at that time was concerned.

I pretended not to be, but I was devastated. We had been shopping my songs for nearly five years. I had been turned down repeatedly. I was almost thirty years old—ancient as far as the music business was concerned. The women who were being signed at that time were in their early teens. Female pop music was very sexualized and youth-oriented. I was neither. I still remember Neil insisting "If they're telling us no, we're on the right track." Bless him.

Then something happened that changed everything for me, related to another thing that was percolating in Allan's life like a burner left on when you leave the house. A few days after Allan turned us down, his fiancée (Jill—I've never forgotten her name) decided she didn't love him enough to marry him. She broke up with him, and that sent Allan to an unfortunate place. Heartbreak had a name, and her name was Jill.

Allan was so down, he took a bit of compassionate leave from work. I can't remember exactly how much time passed. After he got back to A&M, Allan listened to my tape again. He was obviously in a different state of mind. One of the demos on that cassette was called "I Just Don't Love You Anymore," and when Allan heard it with new ears, he got it. He had just experienced a really traumatizing breakup, and now *all* of my songs, which were about love of some description, made sense to him.

Good things come out of bad things. My good thing came out of Allan's bad thing.

Allan called Neil and said, "I have no idea if I will ever sell a Jann Arden record, but I think I understand what she does and hopefully other people will too." I've been with the same record label going on thirty years now, and yes, Allan, we've sold a few million records.

You can never completely know what's going on around you. There are so many intricate moving parts that it's impossible to see them all. I needed faith to stay the course and trust in what I did. It only takes one moment, one decision made by another human being, one random event, to change your life. That moment when Allan listened with his own ears and not with the ears of the industry, and thousands of seemingly insignificant moments just like that one, are what my life—every life—is made of. I can sit and think about what my life would have been like if Jill hadn't broken Allan's heart, but I can't know and I will never know.

I do hug Jill every time I see her at an industry event, though.

"Thanks for screwing Allan over, Jill," I always say. We've had some good chuckles over the years.

But seriously, if that had never happened, I do wonder where I'd be. Singing in my basement?

People always ask me how I was discovered. I tell them that I don't think I've been discovered yet. They always think I'm kidding, but I'm not kidding. My career hasn't been a single big bang; it's been strings of little moments that don't make much sense until you're able to look back at them. I was never able to see what it added up to when I was younger. So much clarity comes with time.

6. Wear your crown to Walmart.

When my mother was alive, I asked her if she ever thought about being young again. I also asked her, if she could go back in time, would she?

She told me she liked where she was now. Being young was hard, she said, because she didn't know anything. "Everything seemed so big when I was young, and when you get older it all seems smaller and more manageable."

Benjamin Button was on to something, I think. Start out old and get younger, bringing all your knowledge with you as you go. *If I knew then.* Alas. I don't know a single person who doesn't wish they'd known the things they know now when they were just starting out. I always say to my friend Theresa that I am surprised we are still alive, because we did so many stupid things. For reals, we say things to each other like this one she says to me: "Remember that time you fell out of your Corvair and your mom had to drive us home and it would only go in reverse?" (A Corvair is a very weird car from the 1960s. I bought one for two hundred bucks when I was sixteen and, yes, I did fall out of that car and lived to tell the tale.)

In interviews I'm often asked, "What would you tell your younger self?" I've given different answers over the years. In my thirties, I leaned towards cautioning my younger self to skip certain parts. Avoid this and go around that. And for God's sake, don't do . . .

My answer now is so much easier.

Jann, I'd say to my younger self, *you're going to go through a giant shitstorm. You're going to be very hard on yourself and feel ashamed and embarrassed. You're going to question your sanity and your worth and your sexuality, and pretty much every decision you're going to make is going to be difficult. You're going to doubt all of it. You're going to spend years being desperately hungover, and you're going to fail epically, but you're going to make it— you're going to thrive, even. I wish I could take away the hard parts, Jann, but then you wouldn't be me, and being me is super fucking great.*

When I think about Allan Reid being dumped and changing his mind about my music in that crazy moment, I shake my head. I marvel at all the unseen bits of whimsy floating through the air that we forget about because we're too busy planning. How in the world could I have ever planned that? Allan sure didn't plan for that. As much as he changed my life, I changed his. We still talk about it to this day—the absurdity of the chain of events and how random it was and yet how deliberate it seemed all in the same breath.

You have to keep going forward even if that forwardness is kind of sideways—sometimes back-wards. Things stop working when you stay still. You've got to keep moving, listening to that inner voice that dares you to be more than you are. The conversation you have with yourself is a lifelong one, so you may as well make it a positive and encouraging one. If you keep repeating negative, hurtful things inside your head, you will believe them eventually.

One of the main reasons I write things down is that it helps me to see my thoughts on a page, where they seem tactile and more real and more manageable.

The longest

you're ever

going to

anyone

is with

conversation

have with

—

yourself —

When I get them out of my head, I see them for what they are. The way I spoke to myself twenty years ago is completely different from the conversation I have with myself now. Like so many other young women, I had a tendency to knock myself down, convince myself of untrue things and make myself feel constant doubt.

That does change.

As I've gotten older, I have been kinder to myself.

I appreciate my body and my mind and my whole self now on a consistent basis.

And you too will feel worthy of your crown as time unfolds. The Crone in you will make you the most beautiful damn crown you've ever seen and you'll wear it to Walmart. Yes you will.

Women these days are rethinking their future in an unprecedented fashion. Smack dab in the middle of their lives, they're completely renovating their careers, their minds, their bodies, their spirituality, their relationships. Dreaded MIDDLE-AGED FEMALES have become one hell of a powerful club.

Gone are the days when we sat and watched the calendar pages flipping towards the inevitable end of our working years. Gone are the days when in middle age we were expected to simply disappear and begin our watch on the wall—putting new ideas and, God forbid, dreams into a drawer somewhere. Women of a certain age used to be expected to step aside for somebody else and let them take over. That never made sense to me. I have never bought into the idea of being past my prime. I don't think there is a prime. In my fifties, I feel better than I've ever felt in my entire life.

Having a purposeful life at any age is what "prime" is. Creating things, discovering things and helping other people do the same will change you. Trying new things is so fantastic.

Middle age. What does that actually mean? It means that you're in the middle, not anywhere near the goddamned end. The middle! Even in a bloody baseball game, the middle is the best part: people go to use the bathrooms and grab another hot dog and a large popcorn. The middle is where it's at, people! Oh, the Middle! I love the middle of everything. Who doesn't like the middle of an ice cream sandwich or the middle of an afternoon nap or the middle seat in an airplane? Okay, not *that* middle. But more often than not, the middle is the shit!

I remember the day, at fifteen, when I sat with a few of my pals as we calculated the year in which we would all turn forty: 2002! How far away that seemed. How would we ever get to be that OLD? There was a lot of laughter and disbelief.

When I think about being forty now, I laugh just as hard, because I was still so young then. At forty I was just beginning to feel I was finding my stride, my wisdom and, I guess, essentially, myself. Forty was the age when I started feeling a small sense of relief that I was going to be okay. It was the age at which the way I thought about my body and my abilities and my weaknesses started to change. My weaknesses took on a whole new meaning when I hit forty. These precious vulnerabilities, which I always felt I needed to hide, started giving me grace where once they had drenched me in shame and fear. ALL THE FEAR.

I would lie in bed the year I turned forty and literally feel my thinking change. I started to speak to myself in kinder and more optimistic ways. I started to cheer myself on, rather than tear myself apart.

The biggest thing I feared as a young woman—aging—turned out to be the thing fuelling my renaissance. Since I had more experiences to draw from, I was able to reach much broader and more complete conclusions. *Becoming wiser is the reward for getting older.* It was an OMG moment for sure.

What feels better than being sure of yourself? What feels better than knowing yourself? What feels better than at last knowing how to look after your physical and mental and spiritual health? For me, nothing feels better.

For such a long time I didn't think getting older was going to be all that useful, to be honest. The glamour and joy of youth is pounded into us at every turn, so that we end up dreading the one thing that holds a hell of a lot of power in real life: wisdom. I remember, at forty, having moments when I thought, "I know how I feel now." I'd passed whole decades not being sure of how I felt, which seems ludicrous to me now. Being able to simply say "I know how I feel" was transformative. I started having a dialogue with my, well, my soul I guess, that was encouraging and uplifting and mature.

I'd always hated the word *mature*. It sounded so dull, like the fun was over. It turns out that couldn't be more untrue.

As an added benefit, my bloody insurance is cheaper. I can crash into things with the utmost confidence and know I'm covered. (I have no intention of crashing into anything, so don't worry.) It makes me think of that great scene in *Fried Green Tomatoes* where Kathy Bates is driving around a parking lot at the grocery store trying to find a space and some cocky young lady zooms in and steals the one Kathy had her eye on. If you've not seen the movie, I highly recommend it. The point is, Kathy makes a good argument for being older and having more insurance and she speaks #truth.

As I got older, the doubt started disappearing, along with that wet blanket of self-loathing. I just accepted doubt and self-loathing when I was young. When we're young, what everybody else thinks is somehow more important and more valid than our own feelings. We wait for other people to tell us if we are good enough, pretty enough, smart enough, valuable enough. Middle age through to our golden years and even beyond really can be something to look forward to, because the passage of time helps us to see our authentic selves.

—

Still, it's hard being a person. I say that all the time, because it's true. I don't think there has been a philosopher in human history who hasn't at some point written something about the key to inner happiness being to know yourself. You don't need me to tell you that. I'll just add that it takes a lifetime to get to know who you are, so don't panic if you think you've run the clock out.

I was very inconsistent in my twenties and thirties. One day I'd be all RAH RAH RAH and the very next morning I would be YOU CAN'T DO THAT, WHAT ARE YOU THINKING? And, of course, with all the negative thoughts came the anxiety and low-grade depression that I knew, even then, was self-induced. I'd handed myself a load of crap and took it at face value. That old adage "Just because you think it doesn't make it true" didn't resonate with any part of me. I believed the bad things I thought, however ridiculous. You don't realize that thoughts are tangible things until you start making yourself feel sick with them.

The way you talk to yourself is unbelievably important. It can make your life easier or harder, and that is a fact. How can you change the conversation going on in your own head? How can you make it more constructive and positive and kind? That's always the question. The answer is that it takes time, because talking trash about yourself is a habit like any other. We get into the habit of doing things a certain way, and that includes the way we communicate with ourselves.

You change that habit one thought at a time. One positive, kind, encouraging thought at a time, that's how.

I believe, I THINK, that I can do anything now, no matter how unrealistic that thing is, however lofty or crazy or unattainable. I'll take my new attitude over not believing in myself any day of the week. Why the heck not? If failing is the worst possible outcome, I welcome that over not trying at all.

It was wonderful to realize I was capable of rewiring myself. By learning through experience about all the things I didn't want, the things I did want became that much clearer.

I do what I say I am going to do now, and I never used to. If I don't think I can do something—if I don't have time or space, or if I just don't want to—I say as much. "I'm sorry, I won't be able to do that." Simple, right? Not always. As a young woman, I didn't follow through on the things I said I was going to do; it was one of my biggest flaws. I was constantly letting myself down, as well as everybody around me. It made me dislike myself a LOT.

Small things are big things. They add up. They string themselves together and make up a life. I thought nothing of saying to my mother, "Sure, I'll iron Dad's shirts when I get home from school," and then not doing it. I didn't care.

I didn't think anything of promising a friend that I'd meet them for a coffee and then calling twenty minutes before we were supposed to get together and cancelling. It didn't dawn on me how those broken promises would build up and choke my self-worth. I wasn't doing that kind of thing every now and then, but all the time. Even though I hated disappointing my mom or my friends, I kept right on doing it well into my thirties, and even into my forties, though I was starting to see the light by then.

Not keeping my word set me back. Not keeping my word made me feel bad about myself. Not keeping my word made people mistrust me. Not keeping my word did not fill me with good energy—it drained me and kept me down. One thing I pride myself on now is that I am unflinchingly reliable. If I say I'm going to do something, I do it. Which proves you *can* change. When you feel like an authentic version of yourself, you navigate life differently. The simple truth was, I was sick of letting myself down.

Those things I didn't follow through on built up inside me until my whole body was a fault line waiting for an earthquake of self-doubt to split me apart—and it did. I drank too much, which was a huge part of my problem, though I denied it for a long time.

I abused alcohol on a regular basis from the time I was sixteen years old. I was a lousy drinker. The first time I had a gulp of rum, I loved it. The feeling was liquid oblivion. It hit my veins like the perfect lover. I felt invincible. Thank God I never got into drugs, because I doubt I would still be alive. I have read many descriptions of what having the first drink or the first hit of a drug feels like. My dad's version of it was one of the most haunting. He said that "people who are alcoholics or drug addicts are practising how to die." That always made me shudder: *people who are practising how to die.* I wish I'd asked him if that was how he felt about it. I guess the unhappiness and desperation in that statement say it all.

Some part of me had the sense to stay away from drugs. Where I grew up, they weren't really a thing, or if they were, I didn't know about it. The only drugs the kids around me used at the time were the marijuana they grew in their parents' basements, that hash oil the rich kid I knew was selling and magic mushrooms.

I never understood the mushroom thing. I remember being at a party in the early eighties and everybody who had done mushrooms was throwing up and then freaking out. It didn't look all that magical. Drinking, on the other hand . . .

But drinking made me let people down. I was forever calling friends and business associates to cancel lunch dates or meetings, not because I didn't want to see them, but because I was hungover. And when I say hungover, I mean really, really sick. Miserably sick. Profoundly sick. The saddest part is that I'd made myself sick.

Most of my friends were in the dark about how much of a problem drinking was for me. I hid my abuse as much as I could. I played down my hangovers when, in reality, I was hungover three or four times a week. The version of me people saw didn't actually exist. I didn't even show her to the ones closest to me. When I was able to come up for air, I was ashamed of my behaviour, but the shame wasn't enough to get me to stop drinking. I kept right on going.

It makes me cringe when I think about those days for too long. I'm still working on forgiving myself, but I am also working on taking in and acknowledging the glory of my accomplishment when it comes to my overall health now. I am so proud of what I've done and where I've come from. I am so fucking proud that I stopped drinking, and I remind myself of that every damn day. I don't know why we feel we can't say those kinds of things to ourselves. Don't ever think you're too far down the tunnel to find your way out. That's simply not true. I am living proof.

And please keep in mind, I did not succeed on the first or second or even the third attempt to stop drinking. It took me a dozen or so times. Don't be hard on yourself. Reload, regroup and try again.

—

So how in hell did I stop, you may be wondering.

I had many "episodes" with my heart health over the years that put me in hospital. I suppose they were heart attacks, but the medical people called them "episodes." Whatever they were, they were scary as all hell, and unbelievably painful. My left ventricle would literally puff itself up so that it was only able to pump a third of what it was supposed to. I was very fortunate that it went back to normal each time after about four weeks, although my overall recovery could last up to a year. It was a slow crawl back to feeling good again.

I actually lost count of how many episodes I had. "This can't possibly have anything to do with alcohol," I would tell myself. But I was never forthright with any of my doctors about how much I drank. Finally, on my last heart-related hospital visit, in 2016, I told the nurse assigned to me in emergency, "I'm drinking a lot." I don't know why I finally admitted it. I didn't want to die, I guess.

The nurse's name was Nancy, and I don't think Nancy has any idea that she saved me. I'm sure Nancy spoke to hundreds of patients in the same calm, reassuring, non-judgmental way she spoke to me.

"You need to care about yourself enough to stop drinking, Miss Richards," she said. "Your heart doesn't like it."

Just like that, I did stop drinking. I feel so grateful for Nancy's words that day.

Good things come out of bad things. Sobriety is now my superpower.

If you've ever looked into a mirror and said to yourself, "I'm drinking too much," you *are* drinking too much.

It's never too late to help yourself. It's never too late to repair old wounds. It's never too late to take responsibility for your actions. It's fucking hard owning up to the things you're doing that aren't good for you. It's hard to be brave, because you have to summon up courage from the most vulnerable part of yourself.

Sometimes life seems like one giant secret. We all walk around hoping that nobody will find out what we're really doing to ourselves and to the people around us. I knew full well when I was off track. I knew when I was not being true to who I was. We all know when we're being less than we can be, because we don't feel right in our body. We fill up with anxiety

and dread, and then we get so used to feeling that way
it becomes our default setting. You forget how great it
is to feel safe and sound in your own body. When
I stopped drinking, I immediately started to feel
more and more like myself.

I am myself again.

I am myself again.

I am myself again.

I kept saying that over and over in my head
because I was so relieved.

I hated myself when I was drinking, I really did.

I LOVE MY SOBER, SUPER-POWERFUL SELF.

There are many reasons why people abuse alcohol.
For me, it was partly because I didn't feel worthy of
good things. I was scared of succeeding—there it is
again—and it was also partly because it made me less
inhibited. Or so I thought when I was drinking. It
turns out I'm far less inhibited sober, which still kind
of blows my mind. Also, how did the thing I disliked
most about my dad, his alcoholism, manage to push
its way into my life?

Sometimes I would be sober for a few weeks and
convince myself that I didn't have a problem, but then

I'd fall right back into it. I know I ruined relationships because of my drinking. I know I damaged my mental and physical health. But I have forgiven myself for all of it. I've forgiven myself, and I haven't for one second felt anything but compassion and love and enormous pride for not giving up on my future or myself.

You mustn't give up on your future self.

I was the curator of all my obstacles. That was a difficult thing for me to accept when I finally came up for air long enough to truly see what I was doing. That's why addictions are so insidious: they don't want you to see your true self. You are not what you did, but what you will do.

For me, the old saying about needing to hit rock bottom was true. My mother used to say about people she knew who were in trouble, "When they finally hit rock bottom, they'll have something to push themselves off of." Hitting that solid bottom of the barrel was my saving grace.

My long failure to be a person of my word— drinking or not—filled me with a lot of confusion. I hated being disappointed in myself. What a vicious circle that can be. Doubt is loud and obnoxious as it yells in your ear, and everybody can feel it emanating off you. I didn't feel as though I could enter a room without the entire place knowing what a fraud I was. When I finally started doing what I said I was going to do, I changed my life. And it wasn't just big things that changed, and it still isn't—it is the tiniest, seemingly most unimportant things. The little things have a huge impact on how you make your way through the world. When I wasn't accountable to myself, things unravelled on a regular basis. When I wasn't authentic, I was almost always unhappy. Self-respect was sorely missing in my life as a young woman. Now my power stems from being a person of my word and being sober. Do what you say you're going to do. You'll experience a huge shift in how you feel about yourself, and how others feel about you as well.

I don't have any easy answers as to how a person comes to respect themselves. I am one of those people who always had self-confidence but very little self-esteem. You'd think those two characteristics can't coexist in the same body, but I'm living proof that they can and do. If you tell yourself something often enough, over a long-enough period of time, it will manifest itself. When I'd finally had enough of sliding downhill, I began to tell myself positive,

It is very

self confindence-

self

possible to have

and ZERO

esteem —

uplifting things. I didn't believe in them wholeheartedly at first, but I kept repeating them. One day a
shard of what I was saying finally seeped into me for
real. It felt like an answered prayer of sorts. Even
though I'm not a particularly religious person, I pray
all the time. When I'm talking to myself, I'm praying.
When I'm wondering about things, I'm praying.
When I'm cheering myself on, I'm praying. When
I'm singing, I'm praying. I pray all day long.

For me, a prayer is a thought that connects me to
the human grid. A prayer is a positive affirmation and
an earnest attempt simply to help myself. If I don't
give a shit about me, how in hell is anybody else going
to give a shit about me? I know that sounds harsh, but
it's true. You have to ask for help, but you have to want
to help yourself as well. Nobody else could stop
drinking for me. I had to do that.

My dad used to say, "First the man he takes the
drink, and then the drink he takes the man." Yes, he
had a drinking problem, but he also knew what was
going on.

My grandmother told me a story when I was young
about an angel bringing an old man who had just died

Every thought
you think —
is a kind of little
prayer ...

to see a beautiful room in heaven—showing the old man the ropes, as it were. This room was the last stop on the tour "before," the angel said, "we take you to Jesus." (Bear with me.) The angel opened the giant, glittering, bedazzling door and led the man inside the biggest room he'd ever seen. It was so unbearably bright the man felt as though he was walking into the sun. Around him were row upon row upon row of beautifully wrapped gift boxes in different shapes and sizes. The angel led the man up and down the rows with a great deal of pride and delight.

"Where are we?" the man whispered. "What is all this?"

The angel stopped and gently rested her shimmering hand on the man's shoulder. "Why, these are all the things you never asked for."

That story has stuck with me all my life. *All the things you never asked for.* I am the WORST person in the world as far as asking for help goes. It's something I've really worked hard to improve on in the last few years. When both my parents got sick in their early seventies, it took me by surprise. To cope with them—to help them cope—I had to reach out to my friends and colleagues and, sometimes, people

I didn't know from an old tire. Asking for help wasn't easy and still isn't easy for me. I'll be struggling with something and then realize that I've shut myself off from my people. It happens without me even knowing it.

What has changed because of my long journey with my parents is that I have made myself aware. I check in with myself all the time. I used to be reluctant to do that because I didn't really want to know what was lurking in my head. Now, I *want* to know. I'm not afraid to see all of it. Sobriety has done that for me too. Clarity is life-altering in new ways every single hour I'm alive. Clarity is everything. Clarity is my new addiction. I want to feel *everything*.

Writing about my mother's Alzheimer's changed my life profoundly. Because of it, I found myself reaching out to others on a massive scale. I surprised myself the first time I posted on Facebook: "Here is what I'm dealing with and I'm scared to death, but here it is." The response to my posts about Mom set me on a path that I couldn't have imagined even a few months earlier.

I didn't think anyone on the planet would care about what my mom and I were going through.

It turned out people did care. My words resonated with thousands upon thousands of people who were struggling and suffering right along with me. Their responses gave me the strength of a whole community. Even on my most difficult days I didn't feel alone, because I knew there were so many other people going through the exact same things in that exact same moment. Because I could put words to what we were all going through, I got to be somebody else's "Nancy." Grief shared is grief lessened.

It has been humbling, to say the least, being able to connect with so many other human beings and share my grief, my troubles and my concerns, and, in doing so, lift the weight that all of those troubles bring.

I do understand the importance of opening myself up to other people by sharing my experiences. But I also am acutely aware of when I need to be on my own. That, too, is new. Finding the balance between being around people and not being around people has been a long journey for me. As much as I am a social person, as much as my job has me surrounded by other human beings in a very intense way, I can't function without a lot of time to myself.

I have to take a minute here to stare at those words I wrote in the first draft of this book: "I can't function without a lot of time to myself."

Little did I know a global pandemic would soon hit the giant pause button on the thing we hold so dear—life—and, for so many, actually take their lives. We all had to stop. The novel coronavirus was the bowling ball and we were the pins, all seven and a half billion of us. I wish we had that weird pin resetter to pick us up and get us the hell out of the way!

There was no way to know how soon we would be spending A LOT of time with ourselves or that we would be doing it for months on end, separated from our friends and extended family members. For those of us single people, it was an extra blow. I was thankful that I had been "practicing"! Living on my own with my thoughts pestering me day and night was something that felt fairly normal to me.

Other things not so much: for instance, the way flour and toilet paper became a currency overnight. If I had been a betting woman, I would have lost the farm on that one. My friend Julie called fast-rising yeast the "new gold," which made me laugh and sort of cry. I've had friends make fun of me over the years because I always have a forty-kilogram bag of flour bending a shelf in my cupboard and alongside a very large jar of yeast. It turned out I was just prepared.

This may feel a little optimistic a spin, but I'm pretty sure we all discovered new, interesting, powerful and unbelievable things about ourselves because of the lockdown—things that might have taken us ten or twenty years to realize had we not been forced to adapt and change and assimilate to a very new way of living. We reached out in all sorts of virtual ways for connection, including making music for each other.

But the catalyst to having a better understanding of who we were, was time spent alone. None of us will ever be the same and I think for the most part that's a good thing. Our aloneness showed us our deepest fears and worries and concerns and anxieties and priorities too. And many of us realized how strong we actually were, how strong we are.

I don't do my best thinking in a group or even with one other person in the house. I can't seem to hear myself when I am around other people. But I didn't know this for the longest time. One of my biggest breakthroughs was realizing that I thrive when I have time alone. Making sure I have enough time on my own lets me be around other people and not want to punch them in the throat or punch myself in the temple.

I know finding time for yourself can be difficult when you have kids and jobs and partners and parents and events and dinners and shopping, and the list goes on. But if I could tell my young self only one crucial thing about living, it's this: *You have to find time to be by yourself. You'll never hear what's going on inside you otherwise.*

It's not as scary as you think it's going to be. Even if you start with only an hour a week, the benefits will surprise you. Don't read, don't draw, don't stare at your phone for that hour. Just sit in a chair or go for a really good walk and think about *yourself.* When you first try this, it'll be unbearably loud in your head, because you've got a lot of things going on that you've likely been avoiding, but it sorts itself out eventually. It really does.

How. Do. You. Feel?

When I was in my twenties and thirties and someone asked me that, I honestly didn't know. Now, when somebody asks me how I am feeling, I not only know, I TELL THEM. And when I ask someone how they are, I listen. It's an opportunity to care about another human being.

I am more creative, more in tune, more flexible, more empathetic and more engaged with life because I spend a lot of time on my own—though I admit aloneness was forced upon me at first, or perhaps I forced it upon myself.

When I think about being on my own at eleven in my parents' basement, I didn't actually want to be down there all alone. I did it for self-preservation. I didn't really know what self-preservation was, but I was young enough not to second-guess the need. (I'm not sure when it is that we unlearn that child-hood trust in ourselves. I'm not sure when doubt becomes our default setting, but it does.)

My eleven-year-old self said, "Get out of harm's way, Jann. Don't be around this mess. Go be where there isn't anybody else." And after a while, spending time alone became a necessity, not a defence mechanism.

A lot of people think they need to spend a pile of dough and head to an ashram in some far-off country in order to have that alone experience. Honestly, you can sit in your damn car on the street or lock the

Time spent alone — is NEVER Wasted

JANN ARDEN

bedroom door for an hour. By all means, if you have a basement, go down there and sit in the chair you've had since 1977 and think about who you are. You don't need to sleep in a parabolic chamber with a crystal on your torso to find enlightenment.

Yes, it can be very daunting, but at some point you're going to have to be by yourself, so I recommend trying it before you're stuck on your own in an elevator on the thirty-seventh floor of a building in downtown wherever. Being alone is important. Being alone is a lot different from being lonely.

I wouldn't be able to do the work I do without alone time.

I wouldn't be able to write a single word, or a song, or come up with an idea, or nurture myself, or grow as a human being without the gift of solitude.

I know there are thousands, if not millions, of people who feel desperately isolated and profoundly alone. Ask anyone what they fear the most and somewhere on their list will be "being alone." But there is a cavern of desperation between feeling lonely and the kind of solitude I'm recommending. If you're feeling loneliness biting at your heels, I hope you'll reach out to a friend, a neighbour, a workmate, a schoolmate, a doctor, and let your feelings be heard. Vulnerability is visibility, and when we can see each other, *really* see each other, life will become easier and better and kinder.

Here are some lines from "The Sound Of," a song I recorded over twenty years ago: "No, I will not lay down—I will not live my life like a ghost in this town. I am not lonely, swear to God, I'm just alone . . ."

7. I couldn't write this
if Dad was still alive.

Life goes by quickly, but I don't need to tell you that. You blink and you're twenty, you blink and you're thirty, you blink and, well, you're not blinking at all because your kids or your friends or your much younger Mediterranean lover are having you cremated. The older I get, the more excited I am about getting older. There, I said it.

My dad shoved his fear of death (and life) deep in the pocket of his work pants or in that drawer in his desk that was always locked, the one my brothers and I learned to jimmy. There was a little wooden peg underneath the drawer that you pinched in slightly and, *bing*, it popped open like a jackknife. I don't know what we thought would be in there—gold bullion or a handgun—but we knew, whatever it was, it wasn't meant for our filthy little kleptomaniac hands.

The first time we pried open Dad's secret drawer was exciting and unbelievably f&%$ing scary. I kept waiting for his infuriated red face to appear in the door frame. He was a domineering, intimidating presence in our house at all times. I felt that he could see everything and hear everything. Very few things got past the man.

Inside the locked drawer, we found a groove filled with old coins from the late 1800s, some lovely ballpoint pens, some packs of cigarettes and a couple of butane lighters. When you turned one of the pens upside down, it made a lady's clothes come off. It was fantastic! We made sure to put everything back exactly where we found it so Dad wouldn't know we'd been into his things.

I don't blame him for wanting to have something that was just his, but how I wanted to take one of those lighters or a few of the coins. I didn't, because I didn't want him coming after me, hollering at the top of his lungs like a maniac.

I didn't know him at all, my dad. I feel such a sense of loss about that. He was either extremely private or extremely selfish, and I still haven't decided which. Perhaps a bit of both. I know that I couldn't have written this book if he was still alive, and I am conflicted about that. I wasn't afraid of him for the last ten or fifteen years of his life, but I was cautious.

I never had a conversation with the guy, ever. Quick jabs of sentences passed between us, as though we were two terrible tennis players never having a decent rally. That was about it. I was uncomfortable when I was alone with him. I felt awkward around my own father, and it hurts my heart to think about that even now. I would be lying if I said otherwise. It was hard to look him in the eye.

I think he was drunk for so much of my childhood that I couldn't change the imprint he left upon my brain. I wanted to like him, but it was hard. There were a few occasions in the nineties when he drove me to the airport, probably so I could save money on parking. It was at least a forty-five-minute trip, and each one of those minutes was uncomfortable. Why was it so hard? Why didn't I ask him things? Why didn't he ask me things? We had a canyon between us, and I hated it.

It's taken me years to understand that I did in fact love him, but how could I like him when he was always mad, always brooding, always sullen? In my memory, he only smiled or laughed when he was drinking. It had to be the perfect amount of alcohol in order for his psyche to let itself go. One drink past that "perfect" place and he'd pick a fight with anyone within striking distance. Which is why I was either outside playing with my pals until the sun went down or down in the basement with the record player spinning constantly.

As I said, good things come from bad things. Music and the great outdoors still keep me going.

Spending my childhood in the trees was magic, it truly was. I wouldn't have traded living in the country for anything. I'm glad technology hadn't found us yet. I'm glad it was still a dream in someone's head, waiting to be thrust upon us unsuspecting throngs.

Anyway, I loved playing outside. I loved using my imagination, and I loved being away from my dad. I'm only sad that it meant being away from my mother too. I know she was relieved that I wasn't around the messy stuff all the time, but I think she would have preferred to be more a part of my day-to-day childhood. She'd call me an urchin from time to time. I didn't even know what an urchin was. I thought it was a sea creature, but apparently an urchin is also a small, raggedly dressed child of the streets. Oh—and it is also a hedgehog, so there you have it. I was very independent because I had to be, and that has served me well.

I've often wondered whether my dad—drunk, sad, grumpy, filled with anxiety—suffered from undiagnosed depression most of his adult life and self-medicated his melancholy with alcohol. Men in general aren't great with taking themselves to the doctor, and my dad certainly wasn't. I can't for the life of me see him admitting to his family doctor, "You know, I'm feeling kind of down and I'm not sure what to do about it." It's heartbreaking to picture him in his chair, closed off, thinking whatever he was thinking and feeling lost in his own life.

I asked Mom on a few different occasions how the hell she managed to stay with him.

"Well, when you were younger," she said, "I couldn't leave because we had the dog, and where in the heck would you have shot your gun?"

I wish I was kidding. She actually said that. It makes me laugh to this day. *Where in the heck would you have shot your gun?* I had a pellet gun with a range of about five feet.

As the years wore on and I kept asking, Mom would simply say that it had gotten to be too late. Where would she have lived, and what would she have done? She didn't want us kids to have to change schools or move to a little city apartment. (Where indeed would I have shot my gun!) We had dogs and two geese and rabbits and a garden—Mom simply couldn't get her head around all the details of leaving that behind.

I get that. But she forfeited her life for his. She served him like a maid their entire marriage. She plunked his dinner in front of him every night, and the only thing I can remember him saying in response was, "That was good, Mother." End of story. He never helped her make a bed or clean a floor or, God forbid, scrub a toilet. He sat in a chair and read a pocket book, and she tolerated it. Yes, he did things outside the house, but it was always on his terms. Though I didn't understand this until I was away from it, until I was older, my mom bears at least some of the blame for where they both found themselves existing.

That was hard for me to accept.

That was hard for me to get my head around.

My mother *chose* not to change anything. She stayed where she was because she was afraid of what change would look like.

I don't want to do that. I don't want that stasis to be part of any more of my relationships. We tend to repeat the patterns we learned in childhood without realizing it, but once you do realize it, it's on you to move, to shift, to alter, to adjust—call it what you will, but don't settle for half a life. I loved my mother, oh my God, but I hate that she martyred herself for anybody, especially her husband—the person who was supposed to carry her when she couldn't carry herself. My mom didn't like confrontation, and I am exactly like her in that regard. I don't like friction or contention or confrontation or arguing. I barely manage discussing.

My parents led separate lives in the same house, the same room, in fact, for almost fifty-seven years. They were alone together. At times this picture of their marriage fills my heart with an unbearable weight. Dad was horribly ill with dementia for the last ten years of their marriage, and she looked after him with an unflinching loyalty. It turned out she gave him the last good years of her own life, given that she was diagnosed with her own Alzheimer's when he died. She scrubbed the diarrhea off the carpeted stairs and the bedsheets and the towels and his constantly soiled trousers. She cleaned up after him and she never complained. She propped him up and bathed him and fed him, and she was tireless.

I was angry with my dad for being sick, for having been careless with his life and his health. But now I realize I myself have walked a mile or two in his shoes, driven by my own anger and frustration. I'm working every day to be forgiving—pushing myself to change the narrative in my head, to move past the mistakes I made and the path I chose during a huge part of my life—and find peace with it all.

But I can be mad about the way my dad was and still do all those things. It's not going to help anybody if I sit here and jot down how good things were. I am who I am because of obstacles, not because of successes. I am the type of person who learns very little from getting it right, and I now believe my dad was very much like me in that regard.

I do have some fond memories of him. He loved movies and he loved reading. He took us to the drive-in every Friday night without fail in the late sixties and early seventies. We'd all pile into whatever crap car he was driving and head to the 17th Avenue drive-in theatre in Calgary. It didn't matter what the weather was like—the dead of winter or the oppressive heat of summer—we'd go to see a movie or two. In summer they started the first one while the sun still hung high in the sky, so you couldn't see much. Dad hung the blown-out speaker on the inside of his window so he could hear the best, and the sound was distorted. I can't tell you how many people drove off after the second feature was over, half-asleep, and ripped the speaker right off the post because they forgot it was there. As for the sound in the back seat, we might as well have been underwater. My brothers and I had to learn to read lips, I swear to God, to follow what was going on, but it was still such a happy time.

My dad lived for the movies, getting lost in the action and the fantasy. My mom enjoyed the movies too—I think because he was so calm for a change. He seemed like the best version of himself when we were parked there on that dirt slope, car pointed at the giant screen. He always let Mom take us inside for snacks—popcorn and huge dill pickles on sticks and fountain pop. I still can't believe he took us to the drive-in so consistently.

Mind you, he always had a stubby bottle of beer between his knees, and he would puff away on one cigarette after another. We three kids would be in the rear of the car, hot-boxed on nicotine fumes. Thank God for that speaker hanging on the window, because at least there was some fresh air coming in.

Even now, I can picture the back of my dad's head. He was so caught up in the stories, the action and the music, he'd laugh out loud, which was such a rare thing. I see him clearly at last: a young man with three kids he didn't have a clue what to do with and could barely support.

I remember Mom sticking us in our pyjamas before we left the house so we'd be ready for bed. I guess not my older brother, but certainly Patrick and me. The feeling of Dad carrying me into the house after the drive-in, through the crisp night air, is something I will think about until the day I die. Something so simple. He couldn't have known how much it would mean to me as a fifty-seven-year-old woman living on without him. I remember feeling safe and secure and without a single worry. It was glorious.

It's getting easier for me to empathize with him as I get older, and that is truly a gift. My dad was just a guy with his own shit. The things I see now, the things I understand, are because of the passage of time. I'm so grateful to have the opportunity to be older.

I have never understood people who lament their birthdays. They will almost always tell you that they wish they could be young again, but only if they knew then what they know now.

Maybe I'm missing a few bricks in my wall, but I prefer the older, more beat-up version of myself. I prefer the lines on my face and the bits and pieces of me that have broken off and now rattle around inside my chest. I prefer my current state of ease and grace and intermittent wisdom. I like the fact that I'm finally at a place where I can breathe in and out without being strangled by self-doubt and constant worry about things that might happen. I like my new steadfastness when it comes to decisions that would have stolen my sleep twenty years ago. I like how I feel about who I am. It's exhilarating.

Power comes with the passage of time, and wisdom comes from failure. I said that already, but I need to say it again.

I feel the Crone in me growing bigger and stronger—the aging, disagreeable hag who lives in the forest, casting spells and planting mysterious seeds that grow into ideas and hopes and dreams and real-life wonders. I feel her magic and her supernatural strength transforming the naive and fearful young woman I was and turning her into a goddess.

I work hard to cherish every single day I have on earth. I really do want to look into a mirror many years from now and see a very old, wrinkled and wise woman looking back at me.

My dad wasn't a big birthday person. I cannot remember a time when he didn't complain about getting older. In his thirties, he talked about not making it to forty. In his forties, he talked about not making it to fifty. That narrative continued right up until the actual end of his life. He officially died of pneumonia, which is apparently one of the best ways to go, but he didn't go peacefully. Can regret be a cause of death? He was full of it. He didn't want to pass over into the light, but maybe my dad's light felt like a train hurtling towards him.

He was raised in a fairly rigid Mormon family. Though he left the church in his early twenties, rebelling against its strict teachings, the rules and regulations his parents lived by, his upbringing dogged him until his dying breath. I think it was half of his battle with the afterlife. My mom hadn't joined his church when they got married, which was a bone of contention with her mother-in-law. I know Dad felt that he had failed his mother, especially, when he left the church. She mourned losing him to the secular world (and my mother) and worried that he wouldn't be saved. She was always telling him it was never too late to come back to the fold and atone for his short-comings. Not a great way to make your way through the world, with your own mother telling you you're basically doomed.

Maybe my dad learned his parenting skills, or lack thereof, from her. My grandmother Crilla was economical and unsentimental and strict. Why she was like that is anyone's guess. I would be comfortable betting the whole farm that it had something to do with her own upbringing and her parents' religious leanings. At some point, you have to break the cycle and start something new. My dad tried.

When I was about ten, my dad told Patrick, Duray and me that we didn't have to go to Sunday school anymore. Since he resented having to go to church, he figured we must too. I never went again. None of us did. Dad told us that he wanted us to figure out our own ideas of faith and spirituality, unhindered by whatever he believed. I've been trying to do that ever since. Maybe he wanted us to have a chance to be happy and not be bound to some ridiculous doctrine that would saddle us with extra layers of guilt and shame. Giving me the freedom to decide what I believed in was one of the best things my dad ever did for me.

My dad was good to his mother despite their often rocky relationship. She came to stay with us a lot when I was growing up. She lived a few hours south of Calgary, in Lethbridge, and Mom and Dad always took us on the road trip to go pick her up. She spent many Christmases with us at our Springbank house, a compact, short and sturdy woman who loved to eat (who doesn't) and who always had a glass of ice water nearby. She had diabetes she managed with insulin, and I'm pretty sure she didn't manage it all that well, since it eventually killed her. Her heart gave out, as hearts do. My dad was broken up about it. Perhaps he felt their fence was never mended and that the things that hung between them would be left unresolved. I can relate.

I don't remember ever having a lengthy conversation with my grandmother either; in that regard, she and my dad were truly similar. For sure he inherited her brooding and dour disposition. Mom would always say, "I might as well have married your dad's mother, they're the same GD person." (Unlike my father, my mom did not swear. She made up swears that were just as effective, though. "GD" was always at the ready, as was "Judas Priest," "For the love of Gord," "Jimminy Christmas" and the always popular "Darn it anyways." Though she did like to say "What the hell" when it came to whether she should have a beer at the end of a long day.)

Grandma Crilla did not laugh. She seldom smiled, except if she was singing about Jesus or cheating at cards or winning at Yahtzee. She could bang away on her upright piano and belt out a hymn like there was no tomorrow. Though she was not a warm person by any means, she let me sit beside her at the piano as she sang at the top of her lungs. She was the first person I ever heard sing live, and I loved it. That was before I retreated to the basement, and may even have been the spark that lit the fire when it came to me and music. For that, I will be eternally grateful.

When I think unkind thoughts about the kind of person she was, I remind myself that she lost her husband, my grandfather Owen, a few months before I was born—her partner, her companion, the father of her children and the primary breadwinner. He was only fifty-six or so when he died—around my age now. Dad spoke so fondly of his father that I know he missed him. Maybe my dad's life would have turned out much differently if his father had lived another twenty or thirty years. Instead, as my dad always said, he worked himself into the grave: "He had about three jobs at one time and he went from one to the next to the next and it killed him." That was about all he would say about it. You had to pry words out of Dad's mouth with the goddamned jaws of life.

I actually never heard Dad say a disrespectful word about either of his parents. He loved them, but felt unworthy of their love at every turn. He felt as if he let everybody down no matter what he accomplished, and lived his life afraid and apprehensive and unsure, as many of us do. Maybe Dad felt just as awkward trying to talk to his parents as I did trying to talk to him.

Time has given me the clarity that only comes when the days and the months and the years pile up on each other so you can stand on top of it all and have an unobstructed view. I am starting to forgive him for being absent, even for being mad all the time. I realize now that he wasn't mad at us kids or at Mom; he was mad at his own life. We took his uncontrollable temper and his silences so personally. I used to think he didn't love me, but he loved us all profoundly. I think he found that so hard to express because he always felt unworthy of our love. That has been the real discovery for me.

I remember the day I realized that Mom and Dad had been kids like me at some point, struggling to understand life in the very same way I was. I was thirty-nine years old, and the revelation rushed past me like a runaway horse. Until then, I guess I'd assumed that my parents were on the planet only to facilitate my every want and need. It hadn't dawned on me that they were these real, living, breathing, vulnerable, fragile human beings who were probably as scared as I was about life. And they weren't just dealing with their own crap, they had to take on the responsibility of the three of us kids, who were needy, ever-wanting, constantly hungry, endlessly questioning and unsure. (There are days when I feel I'm ill-equipped to take care of my five-pound dog.) We thought our parents were supposed to hold all the cards, have all the answers, know the secrets to how the magic tricks worked. They didn't.

I am finding forgiveness in my memories of my dad more often now. Time is wise. Time is even-tempered. Time brings things into a bright and steady light.

I am going to keep working on being gentle and non-judgmental with my father's spirit. Even though he is no longer physically here, I am chipping away at the wall that Dad and I built between us over the years, tearing it down brick by brick, for both our sakes. We are all flawed, and that's half the fun, isn't it? Or it is until we implode, and then not so much. We do things that aren't good for ourselves or anybody around us, and we keep on doing them. I've hit pause on that cycle when it comes to my parents, and am glad of it.

No one taught Mom and Dad how to be parents. No one gave them a book that said, "This is what you need to do." Nobody showed up on the weekends to give them a break or make them a meal or cheer them on. They were on their own and winging it, as most parents do. I think I would rather stand naked in a mall parking lot at Christmas than be a parent. It's not easy raising a family; it strikes me as twenty years, at least, of full-on combat mode. Every family is different, and if you're looking for what a normal family is supposed to look like, well, you're kidding yourself. There is no normal. Every single family is unique.

I could have been a much better daughter. I created my own secret world and was reluctant to let anybody into it. For a long time I kept my parents out of much of my life. When you're growing up, it feels as though time shows you only what you need to know in the moment (or maybe just after). It's cruel that way, letting you stumble along like a three-legged dog. "If I knew then," we say to ourselves every time we think about the obstacles we faced, those sharp-toothed challenges that ripped into us and, eventually, made us better. Still, we wish we'd had the tools back then that we have now, so we could have avoided the trips and subsequent falls.

But you can't skip the hard stuff to get to the easy stuff. We'd all be vacuous drones if that were the case. I think being broken makes us interesting. I'm broken in many ways, but I've put all of the busted-off pieces of myself to good use. How can you relate to anyone else's pain if you haven't experienced pain yourself?

Yes, for much of my youth Dad was a crap parent. He was hard on us because he was hard on himself. I get that now. It doesn't make it right, but I can't spend the rest of my life dragging all of the times he disappointed me up a mountain. I'm working my way back to loving him.

Being in my fifties has given me permission not to take on anybody else's stuff anymore, and certainly not his. I can remember that feeling of carrying around my dad's guilt. I didn't have the words to express it then, but that's what it was. I was sixteen and seventeen years old and carrying around my dad's addiction. I carried it to school, I carried it into friendships and, later in life, I carried it into my career and my own intimate relationships. I didn't even know I was doing it.

And with Dad's guilt, I also carried my mother's grace and serenity, her easygoing good-heartedness.

The polarity in their parenting somehow gave me
a glimpse of a world I needed to see. They could not
have been more different from each other. They made
their way through life from opposite directions.
I don't know whether we would have all been better
off if she had left him, but I'm glad she didn't. I'm
glad we stayed in the house in the country with the
dogs and the trees and the small schools. There were
perfect summer days, and the memory of them can
lift me up like nothing else.

It's still not easy for me on some days to find
peace and forgiveness for things that happened
nearly forty years ago. But those days now feel more
like a challenge than a heartbreak. I feel myself
getting stronger every single time I let old
things go.

The Crone living in the forest has taken me
over, and I don't mind one bit. Time has smoothed
the edges of bad memories; it's taken the sting and
the bite out of things that used to overwhelm me.
It's interesting to be able to understand the necessity
in the shitty things that happened to me, and the
purpose of all the mistakes and missteps and things
I didn't seem to get right. Maybe I did get them right?

Maybe that was exactly what was supposed to have happened.

I think *destiny* is just another word for *determination*. I am where I am because I didn't quit. I also had people around me who didn't quit on me. They weathered it all, and remained ever so steadfast. My gratitude for the amazing people in my life is boundless and indivisible.

8. The best relationship I ever had.

I am often asked what success means to me, and my answer hasn't changed a word over the last thirty years. My friendships are my greatest successes.

When I was younger, I thought I had a lot of friends, and I did have a lot of friends. But as time marched on, those numbers were reduced to a small group of incredible souls. And so it should be. In order to have a good friend, you need to be a good friend. Friendships require tending, like anything else that grows.

If you make time for the people you love, they will make time for you. Reciprocity is all. If you're around people who do anything but fill you up, you may need to think about the value and integrity of your relationship with them. My friendships are my most important assets, so I guard them ferociously. I expect a lot from my friends, and hope that they expect just as much from me.

At this point, however, I have learned to weed out the people in my life who want something from me. To need someone and want something from them isn't a bad thing, except when it's a one-way street—when that needy person hasn't ever shown up for you, never mind themselves. This one "old" friend of mine texted me out of the blue not so long ago and asked:

A) Could they borrow my truck?
B) Would I be able to drive?
C) Could I help them move, because they'd been evicted?
D) Did I have any spare tickets to one of my concerts?
E) Would I be a reference to help them get their new place?

and

F) (finally, for fuck sakes) How was I doing?

I am not kidding when I tell you that I didn't know who was texting me.

"Who is this?" I texted back.

"Seriously? LOL, it's blah blah blah," they replied.

"Oh hey, I didn't recognize your number . . ."
BECAUSE I HAVEN'T HEARD FROM YOU IN TEN
YEARS, EVER SINCE YOU STOOD ME UP THREE
HUNDRED TIMES. SERIOUSLY, LOL.

So what do you think I did?

NONE OF THE ABOVE.

The version of me from back when I'd last
seen this person would have done all of it, because
I would have felt bad. Obligated, somehow. Feeling
bad or obligated is not a good reason to do anything,
especially when it comes to bailing somebody out
who is a complete dingbat. A part of me felt bad for
them, because it sucks being stuck in a heaping,
steaming pile of chaos, but their problems weren't
mine to solve. Being where I am in my life—being of
a certain age—made that fact perfectly clear.

Crones don't let anybody take advantage of them,
and I love that. Crones will say, "Sadly, I can't lend
you a truck, or help you move, or be your reference
for your new place, because I don't think that would
be good for me right now."

Crones will wish you well and tell you to get your
shit together.

I love being a Crone.

Trust me, I have helped dozens of people move, and every single one of those people has helped to move me—and I hate moving more than anything else in the world. I mean, it's right up there with menstruating and thinking you're pregnant at fifty-one years old.

I've helped them anyway, because they're my dear-heart, darling friends. When I was still eating poultry, they also lured me with the promise of a bucket of KFC and a cold beer at the end of all the hardship. I don't do either beer or chicken anymore, and I don't know if I'd move someone for vegan chicken strips and kombucha. I'll have to ruminate on that one.

Still, no matter what is going on in my life, if one of my friends needs me, I'm there. I've learned how to be a better friend over the years, I think. I've learned it's okay to be vulnerable and honest, and I've learned to lean on my friends when I can't do things on my own.

My mom used to say, "You become who your friends are." That resonates with me now more than ever. The people I have surrounded myself with have had everything to do with my wellness and my happiness. I don't know what I would do without them; I can't imagine my life or my future without these human beings who make everything seem worthwhile. My friendships have never been more solid or more secure or more real.

My friendships are the best "relationship" I've ever been in.

I think women, especially, are handed this idea that they are not complete beings if they aren't in a significant relationship—that we're not whole without a partner. I have felt more complete, more myself, in the last three years of being on my own than I ever felt being with someone. I hate even admitting it, but I wasn't single for thirty years. I never came up for air. If I wasn't overlapping relationships, I was in a new one right on the heels of one that was ending. I couldn't stand the idea of not being involved. I didn't think I could manage. I didn't think I'd feel I was measuring up somehow.

I can't blame it entirely on my drinking, but drinking certainly had a lot to do with it. My last relationship sputtered and staggered and crawled

along for the last five of the ten years we were
together, because both of us were not looking after
ourselves. I'll just leave it at that. I got sober and I got
single and I have stayed single since I quit drinking.

My dad used to make a joke about how he drank
in self-defence, but I can't remember the punchline.
Maybe it doesn't need one. Maybe I was drinking in
self-defence too, which couldn't be more pathetic.
Actually, now that I think about it, he also had a joke
about marriage: "Jann, the worst marriages don't end
in divorce, they don't end." I guess that's kinda
funny. (My parents were together almost sixty years.)

For a long time, I thought if I just kept thrashing
around, moving bad habits from one place to
another, I'd never have to deal with any of them.
I had myself convinced that it was working. Honestly,
it amazes me what I could talk myself into. My life—
my problems, my shortcomings, my relationships,
my broken promises to myself, never mind to anyone
else—was this spinning merry-go-round I couldn't
get off. I wanted to be okay on my own, I wanted to be
"whole" on my own, I wanted to be "happy" on my
own, but in order for all that to start happening,
I needed to get out of my own damn tornado.

What do they say about the eye of the storm? It's so quiet in there you can't imagine the shit flying around you. I think that's why people stay put. In order to change things, you have to own up to how much of the shit belongs to you. You have to look long and hard at things you don't want to see to have a shot at changing them. Sometimes the devil you don't know isn't as bad as the devil you *do* know, and I will never let anybody tell me any different. What I mean by that is, making changes and trying out new things and moving forward might well entail a whole new idea of what the negative things in your life are, but if the fear of going into unknown territory is going to keep you running around in the same old circle, I would highly recommend taking a chance on yourself and embracing change. The devil you do know is a giant pain in the ass, and he's trying his very best to make you doubt yourself.

I know that it's in my character to keep going no matter how dismal things are or how hard things are or how often I don't get it right. I've come to the conclusion that this is what lies at the heart of a human life. It is not going to be easy and, when it is easy, most of us make it harder on purpose!

It makes me laugh when I look back at periods in my life when things were just ticking along. Everything seemed calm and I was content, even on the brink of happiness, and then I would throw a wrench into the wren house, as my mother used to say. I would love to tell you that I *always* learn from my mistakes, but sadly, that's not true. Since I don't think I will ever stop trying new things, I will always risk hitting the ditch.

You are not what you did, you are what you will do. I stress this again, because so many of us hang on to past glories. We hang on to a past we see through rose-coloured glasses that have been taped and glued together about four million times. You can't live there. You can't be happy there. You can't be real there.

You've got to be where you are, not where you were. That's why I always want to be doing new things and learning new things and meeting new people; it's what makes me excited and inspired and satisfied. I think the fact that I've always wanted to go where I've never gone helped to get me out of that spinning mess I'd created.

Getting my health back on track has been an enlightening, fulfilling experience too. I have never felt better than I do now. Yes, there is a huge part of me that wishes I had done it sooner, but that's not the way life works. You do things when you do things. I try not to be hard on myself, and every time I'm tempted to beat myself up, I remind myself that at least I didn't give up. Every time I failed at achieving sobriety, I was still inching forward. I was making progress. I was thinking about positive change. It was on my radar. I wasn't NOT thinking about it. That seems like a small thing, but decades can go by NOT thinking about your issues. If you're failing, you're trying. And if you're thinking about trying, well, that's something—it really is. Change will pester you until you take the first step.

In the last three years, I have gotten more things accomplished and have been more creative and imaginative than I've ever been in my life. My number one focus has been to stay true to my sobriety; my well-being has become my career. One step at a time, one alteration at a time, one encouraging word to myself at a time, I've kept moving forward, backwards, sideways—I've simply kept moving. When I open my eyes in the morning, I wrap myself in gratitude and I find goodness in small things. I am happy to be alive, no matter what life throws at me. I know I can do anything and I know that I have people around me whom I can count on.

I AM SO GRATEFUL. It's become a way of life for me. I don't ever NOT think about gratitude, and I make a conscious effort to fill myself up with its abundance. I want what I have and don't dwell on what I don't have. Good health and friendships are at the heart of that gratitude. I don't want to take away from the importance of my career and what that brings to my life, but I wouldn't enjoy any of it if I didn't have the trifecta of gratitude going on. Health, friendships, career. IN THAT ORDER.

I try not to be hard on myself, and I know it's not always an easy thing to do. You've got to recognize those moments when the universe is giving you an opportunity to shift your whole life around. I was so good at ignoring those moments. I was good at ignoring them for about thirty years.

The hospital visit and my interaction with Nurse Nancy was my "This is it" moment, the point at which something big broke off inside me and I was ready to cry uncle. (I remember doing that as a kid, screaming "Uncle!" at the top of my lungs when my brother was sitting on my face, threatening to fart.) As much as Nancy was the push I needed, I actually made a choice to help myself. And trust me, I was scared.

After about a month of sobriety, I started to feel like someone I used to know and used to like. I started losing weight immediately, because alcohol has a shit-pile of calories and being drunk made me eat a mountain of crap. When the weight began to come off and I was feeling better, I started moving. When I started moving, I started sleeping better. When I started sleeping better, my depression lifted and my anxiety lessened and my world began to shift into what I can only describe as a state of joy and hopefulness.

There are so many clichés about taking things one day at a time, because there is so much truth in that idea. I will never drop my guard when it comes to drinking; I will always exercise caution. It's easy to find yourself right back at the beginning of bad behaviour. I will always have a problem with alcohol. I am not cured. I have simply stopped doing something that hurt me. If I had a drink after a hundred years of sobriety, I would end up abusing it and ruining my life—again.

I still have days when I deal with a mountain of shame. I wake up and that shame is waiting for me on my nightstand. I haven't erased my past by any stretch of the imagination, but I have incorporated all of those disappointing pieces of myself into a very fierce and determined human being. I want to be happy, and if I'm gonna be dragging all of this shit around with me, it's going to be on my terms.

The blunders (maybe blunder-wonders) are important pieces of my puzzle. These are all the experiences that have led me to exactly the place where I am standing now. The Crone in me doesn't mind sifting through them and finding purpose in all the things I didn't get right. The Crone in me always points out the obvious. She says, "Jann, if you hadn't done that, you wouldn't have done this . . ."

You have to take the time to tell yourself these things. You have to take the time to be gentle with your own heart. When I was at last able to wrap gratitude around my mistakes, it was life-changing. I am working on not punishing myself over and over again for the old things I used to drag up just to hurt myself, because, well, I don't know why. When I actually deal with old wounds thoughtfully, they hurt me less and have less power over my present self. I have a Crone inside me now, and she is not one to be screwed with.

We are the only species that punishes ourselves in such a fashion. (Well, dogs do too, but we programme them to feel guilty, so it's pretty much our fault.) Humans will summon a certain day from a cluttered, filthy room in our brain, and we will throw it out onto the kitchen table and purposefully beat ourselves with it. It doesn't make a lick of sense to me, but it's what we do.

As I've gotten older, I've been easier on myself, and that is such a blessing. I am grateful the years have rounded off the jagged edges that used to snag bits of my thin skin and make me bleed. The passage of time has enabled me to be fair with myself.

And why not?

The Crone in me rejoices, because she's not going to be a martyr anymore.

She's not going to linger in the middle of an awkward conversation, she's going to walk away.

She's going to stand up for what she believes in and she's going to speak her mind.

She's not going to apologize for things she's not responsible for.

She's not going to be ashamed of her incredible, strong, resilient body that has been put through more crap than anybody should be put through and still delivers loyalty and steadfastness.

She's not going to stay in relationships that aren't loving and thoughtful and uplifting, and I mean any relationship, not just the ones where you're naked with the other person. In fact, the Crone doesn't need to be in a relationship. She is strong standing right where she is, on her own, breathing in and out on the top of a mountain, owning every single thing she's ever done.

She's not going to be taken advantage of or threatened or bullied or barked at or spoken to in anything less than a respectful tone. Becoming a Crone gives you the sense and the stability and the power to be who you are.

Trust your heart

Even when I'm at the end

GROWING OLDER IS not what it used to be when I was young. We've changed the narrative completely. Fifty years old for our grandmothers was not the fifty or sixty or seventy or eighty years old that we are experiencing now. We walk deeper into ourselves and our power with every passing year. We have the knowledge and the wisdom to take care of ourselves and to nurture our spirits. We know what we don't want. We know what we do want. I want to be responsible for myself.

You are not ever going to hear me complain about growing older. I am fully prepared for things to change and move and drop and sag and shrivel and tighten and give out. I really am. But I have made so many changes in how I live that I think all those things aren't going to be half as bad as I thought they would be. I am looking after my "old" self, actually my "future" self, right this minute. I'm giving my old self an opportunity to be the best possible version of me.

You can change what's coming. You do have control over a lot of things. Look after yourself. Really look after your body. Give it a chance to get old.

Feed it some decent food!

Have a cup of tea instead of a glass of wine.

Walk somewhere instead of just thinking about walking somewhere.

Get up. Move. Breathe.

Forgive *everything*. I mean that.

Hanging on to old wounds—old you-done-me-wrongs, old you-broke-my-hearts, ancient you-screwed-me-overs—will only sink you.

The *Frozen* movie has ruined the saying "let it go" for the rest of time, but I'll say it anyway: let it go. Let it all go.

Falling down is just as important as getting up, because if you're falling down that means that at some point you *were* standing up, and that's saying something.

Get out there and fail!

There is so much love in the world. There is so much good.

Smile at people you pass. Even if they don't smile back, they'll feel that beam of goodness and they'll think about it all day: "Why did that person smile at me?"

I am going to fuck up going forward, I know, but it'll be because I'm trying to be better.

I could have done better with my dad. Our broken relationship still bothers me, and maybe it always will. When I think about it, Dad said some insightful, meaningful things to me in my lifetime, and one of them concerned going to college. I must have been eighteen, at most nineteen. I didn't know what courses to take, because I didn't know what I wanted to do. I was much more frightened than I let on. We were all sitting at the dinner table; it was a rare night when he was home to have a meal with the rest of the family, so it was already kind of weird.

He was asking me about college and the other students and about the parking—yes, the parking— and I was so taken aback. "Is he asking me a question? Is he talking to me?" I thought he was going to be mad, because he always seemed mad, but here he was, summoning up some spark of interest in me.

I'm sure my mother was just as shocked as I was. Anyway, I'm making this story much longer than it needs to be. The point is that he said something that has stayed with me: "Well, it's good that you're going to school again," he said, "because you'll sure as hell find out what you don't want to do."

That has been such a theme in my life: doing things only to find out that I don't want to do them. I am going to continue to fail in just that way because I am going to continue to throw myself out there—into adventure and risk and love and joy and happiness and bliss and new experiences that scare the ever-living hell outta me.

All of this is so unexpected—this getting-older, middle-aged business. I was one of those twenty-five-year-olds who dreaded getting older. I wondered what I would be doing with my life and whom I would be doing it with. I worried about being wrinkled and stagnant and complacent and marginalized and somehow brittle. I didn't know if I'd be working or retired, or if I'd be valued by a society that seemed to have little time for women who were over thirty-five, women who had lost their curb appeal and their usefulness.

I look at my face these days and I see someone who has been true to herself and true to her friend-ships and her work and her community. A woman who has made art in a world that is often cruel and unkind. I look at myself with a sense of pride and accomplishment and true appreciation. No matter how long I live, having had the chance to be here at all has been superb.

I will always feel that I am at the beginning. Even when I'm at the end.

The Crone in me is driving now, the sage woman of the forest who doesn't care about the lines or the scars or the divots or the lumps or the veins.

She's on the move, walking calmly into the next sunrise.

Acknowledgements

Thank you

    For support and kindness that goes beyond everything . . .

    Bruce Allen and the BAT team.

    Chris Brunton.

    Nadine Beauchesne.

    Anne Collins.

    Alkan Emin.

    Nigel Stoneman.

JANN ARDEN is a singer, songwriter, broadcaster, actor, author and social media star. The celebrated multi-platinum, award-winning artist catapulted onto the music scene in 1993 with her debut album, *Time for Mercy*, featuring the hit single "I Would Die for You." A year later she had her international breakout hit, "Insensitive." She has written four books, the most recent being the Canadian bestseller *Feeding My Mother: Comfort and Laughter in the Kitchen as My Mom Lives with Memory Loss.* A multiple Juno Award–winner, Jann continues to record and tour; in 2020 she was inducted into the Canadian Music Hall of Fame. She is also the star of her own hit TV sitcom, *Jann*, which debuted in 2019 and will air a new season in 2020, and is the host of the weekly *Jann Arden Podcast.*